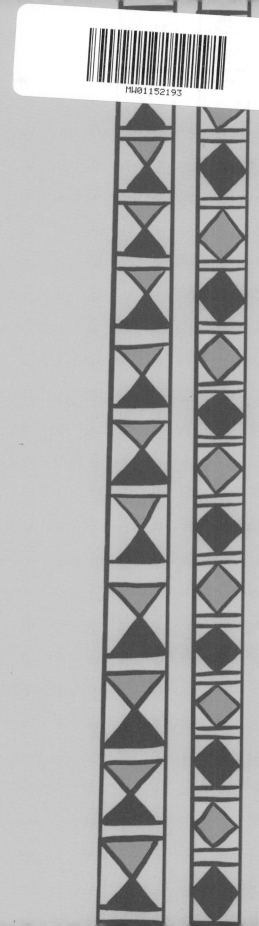

GURSHA

GURSHA

Timeless Recipes for Modern Kitchens,
from Ethiopia, Israel, Harlem, and Beyond

Enjoy!

BEEJHY BARHANY

with Elisa Ung

Photography by Clay Williams
Illustrations by Eden Yilma

B. Barhany

Alfred A. Knopf | New York | 2025

THIS IS A BORZOI BOOK PUBLISHED BY ALFRED A. KNOPF

Text copyright © 2025 by Tevletz Barhany-John
Photographs copyright © 2025 by Clay Williams
Illustrations copyright © 2025 by Eden Yilma

www.aaknopf.com

Knopf, Borzoi Books, and the colophon are registered trademarks of Penguin Random House LLC.

Photo on page 229 courtesy of Hava Tizazu. Copyright © Hava Tizazu.

Library of Congress Cataloging-in-Publication Data
Names: Barhany, Beejhy, author. | Ung, Elisa, author. | Williams, Clay (Photographer), photographer. | Yilma, Eden, illustrator.
Title: Gursha : timeless recipes for modern kitchens, from Ethiopia, Israel, Harlem, and beyond / Beejhy Barhany with Elisa Ung ; photography by Clay Williams ; illustrations by Eden Yilma.
Description: New York : Alfred A. Knopf, 2025. | Includes index.
Identifiers: LCCN 2024013756 (print) | LCCN 2024013757 (ebook) | ISBN 9780593536674 (hardcover) | ISBN 9780593536667 (ebook)
Subjects: LCSH: Cooking, Ethiopian. | Cooking, Israeli. | Jews, Ethiopian—Food. | LCGFT: Cookbooks.
Classification: LCC TX725.E84 B37 2025 (print) | LCC TX725.E84 (ebook) | DDC 641.5963—dc23/eng/20240327
LC record available at https://lccn.loc.gov/2024013756
LC ebook record available at https://lccn.loc.gov/2024013757

Some of the recipes in this book may include raw eggs, meat, or fish. When these foods are consumed raw, there is always the risk that bacteria, which is killed by proper cooking, may be present. For this reason, when serving these foods raw, always buy certified salmonella-free eggs and the freshest meat and fish available from a reliable grocer, storing them in the refrigerator until they are served. Because of the health risks associated with the consumption of bacteria that can be present in raw eggs, meat, and fish, these foods should not be consumed by infants, small children, pregnant women, the elderly, or any persons who may be immunocompromised. The author and publisher expressly disclaim responsibility for any adverse effects that may result from the use or application of the recipes and information contained in this book.

Cover photographs by Clay Williams
Cover design by Anna B. Knighton

Manufactured in China
First Edition

In loving memory of my mother, Azalech Ferede;
my grandparents Ferede Shankur and Bezabesh Worku;
and my aunt Tekavesh Ferede.

CONTENTS

CHAPTER 1 **MAKEDA'S KITCHEN**

CHAPTER 2 **BREAD**

CHAPTER 3 **SUNRISE SUSTENANCE**

CHAPTER 4 VEGETABLES

CHAPTER 5 LEGUMES AND GRAINS

CHAPTER 6 · MEAT AND FISH

143 Doro Wot / Derho Tsebhi / *Spicy Chicken Drumstick Stew*
144 Vered's Doro Wot / Derho Tsebhi / *Whole Chicken Stew*
145 Doro Wot Alicha / *Golden Chicken Drumstick Stew*
146 Sega Tibs / Sega Tibsi / *Tender Sautéed Beef*
147 Doro Tibs / Derho Tibsi / *Sautéed Chicken with Butter and Herbs*
148 PORTRAIT Asefash Mesele: "They Will Come One Day"
151 Berbere Stuffed Peppers with Ground Chicken and Bulgur
152 Schnitzel / *Aromatic Breaded Fried Chicken*
153 Kai Wot / Zigni / *Traditional Spicy, Hearty Beef Stew*
154 Rishan's Kai Wot / Sega Tsebhi / *Israeli-Influenced Spicy, Hearty Beef Stew*
155 Kitfo / *Beef Canapés*
156 Beg Wot / Begi Tsebhi / *Holiday Lamb Stew*
159 Yemenite Chicken Soup
160 Assa Wot / Assa Tsebhi / *Shabbat Fish Stew*
162 Spicy Tomato Tilapia
163 Berbere Fried Fish
167 Injera Fish Tacos

CHAPTER 7 · DRINKS AND PASTRY

171 Buna / Bunn / *Coffee for Prosperity*
174 PORTRAIT Mehrata (Malka) Lemlem Avraham:
Peace and Prosperity
177 Telva / Entati / *Flaxseed Drink*
179 Shahi / Shai / *Ethiopian Spiced Tea*
180 Tej / Mes / *Royal Honey Wine*
183 Suff Drink / *Sunflower Seed Drink*
184 Spris / *Tricolored Layered Smoothie*
187 Sorrel (Hibiscus) Concentrate
190 Redd Foxx Cocktail
193 Kaffa Martini
194 Malawach / *Flaky Flatbread*
197 Legamat / *Fresh Sudanese Doughnuts*
198 Himbasha / Ambasha / *Ashenda Cake with Honey and Cinnamon*
200 Ethiopian Barbecue Corn Bread
201 Collard Greens and Cabbage Bourekas

CHAPTER 8 **HOLIDAYS, CELEBRATIONS,
RITUALS, AND MENUS**

GURSHA

INTRODUCTION

Welcome, my honored guest. In the beautiful village where I grew up in Ethiopia, my family would have considered it a blessing to welcome you to our home. After all, we believed there was no such thing as people we didn't know. To us, every visitor represented an opportunity to prepare *bunn* (coffee) and a meal. As my grandmother always reminded us, this tradition was at the heart of our story as Ethiopian Jews, tracing all the way back to our forefather, Abraham.

Together, we'd enjoy a bountiful meal of the corn and cabbage that grew on our farm, served with stews of lentils and chickpeas that had simmered for hours.

As our guest, you would receive the best piece of chicken from our aromatic chicken stew, doro wot, wrapped in injera flatbread and placed directly into your mouth: an intimate gesture that symbolizes love, friendship, and respect. This is the cherished practice we know as *Gursha* in Amharic—or *haregot* in my native Tigrinya—a word that means "mouthful," and a ritual we perform at the most important times in our lives.

The next morning, we would rattle some green coffee beans around a pan, and when they took on a dark brown hue, grind and roast them into coffee. We would offer you a dish of kolo snack mix, or hanza bread. We might mix up a hearty porridge or a stew of fava beans.

This was the Ethiopia childhood I knew: Abundant. Generous. Food rooted in meaning and ritual.

Since those bucolic days, I've lived all over the world. My family risked our lives on a harrowing journey to Sudan, en route to our promised land of Israel. I then spent most of my teenage years on a kibbutz in Israel before moving to the United States and starting a restaurant in Harlem.

The recipes in this book are the dishes that I have treasured over the journies in my life. Many are traditional Ethiopian staples, while others pay tribute to those who helped my family and me on our journey—particularly Sudanese and Yemenite dishes. Others show how my family melded our cooking with Israeli favorites, or honor famous African Americans and other American cooks who inspired me once I settled in Harlem.

It's my honor to help feed you, my fellow traveler, and to help fill your kitchen with the same heady aromas enjoyed by my family.

MY PROMISE TO YOU

What do you need to cook Ethiopian food? Garlic. Ginger. Onions. Just three basic items, widely found around the world, are the foundation of what you need to make delicious Ethiopian meals. While our seasoning, berbere, can also be widely found in grocery stores, I will teach you to make your own version that's just as good as mine, and I hope that these recipes inspire you to see all the ways it can enhance your cooking.

No matter where I've lived, I've always been able to make Ethiopian food. And the more and more I learn about food around the world, the more I realize that Ethiopian cuisine deserves more recognition, and remains as accessible, versatile, and timely as it was when I was growing up in Tigray.

To my delight, many of the heady stews, ancient grains, and cooking methods used by my ancestors have become trendy again. I've always found ways to adapt these ancient foods to my own modern kitchen—I particularly love using my food processor and other tools to cut hours off the preparation of these dishes, and I'm delighted to report that many of these modern conveniences actually improve them.

Each recipe includes the name for the dish in Amharic, English, and in some cases, my native Tigrinya, which is spoken in Ethiopia's Tigray region.

As I teach you to make these recipes, I'll share with you the stories of my people, the Beta Israel Ethiopian Jews. While we are smaller in numbers and not as widely known as many other groups of Ethiopians or Jews, we have so much to offer the world through our cuisine, flavors, cooking techniques honed over generations, and the naturally healthful and nutritious nature of our dishes.

We Beta Israel persevered through many years to get to this point in history, and as you make our delicious food, you'll see how it represents our courage, strength, and fortitude. Ashkenazi Jews may celebrate the Shabbat with challah and matzah ball soup, while I do it with dabo (bread) and doro wot. We are all striving to do the same thing, to celebrate our unique Jewish identity. For years, I've seen that whenever I introduce people to the smells and tastes of Ethiopian Jewish culture, they are always eager to learn and taste more.

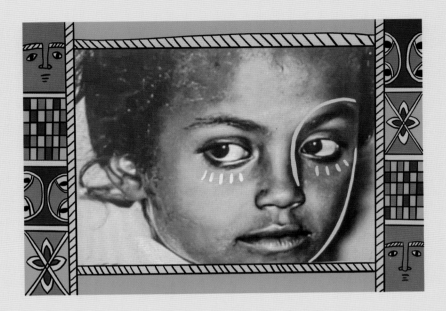

MY JOURNEY FROM ETHIOPIA TO HARLEM

At four years old, perched in my favorite fruit tree, I gazed upon lush, sprawling fields dotted with color: orange pumpkins, crimson tomatoes, and delicate wild greens sprouting up everywhere. I loved to inhale the damp aroma left from a long rain, scurry down the tree, and race into the cornfields, the cornstalks rising far over my head.

Three generations of my large extended family lived together on this land in Ethiopia's Tigray region, as they had for centuries. Our home proudly sat in the seat of the capital in the ancient trading empire of Aksum (Axum). As the first grandchild of my generation to arrive, I was doted on: My grandparents gave me my own goat, a spotted brown and gray animal that I often tried to ride, much to its dismay. My aunt braided my hair, but I always tried to wiggle out of her insistent hands to run off to my next adventure, greeting relatives as they walked by.

If you happened upon my family as we were preparing for the most sacred of days—the Sabbath—you'd see us abuzz with excitement. On Thursday, you'd smell the heady scents of stews simmering and dabo baking. As it became dark on Friday, you'd see us all slip down to the river just before sundown to bathe and purify ourselves, then put on our best white, embroidered dresses. You'd hear a horn blow, the beat of drums, and see our communal walk to the synagogue—a huge, round building where we recited and read from the Orit (Scriptures), heard the Kabbalat Shabbat (blessings), and prayed. We presented our offerings to the Qess (rabbi), and he would bless each household's dabo, our version of challah, and cut off a portion to give to someone in need. Then we took the remainder back to our homes for our weekly Shabbat meal of vegetables from our fields, served over the mesob, the communal basket that we used as a table.

Saturday was also a time for leisurely meals and reflection, giving thanks, and strictly observing the Sabbath: no climbing trees or diving in the river, just enjoying each other's company. At night, I went to sleep knowing I would wake up to the sights, sounds, and aromas of this idyllic place.

The Land of Milk and Honey

That all ended when my grandmother woke me up in the middle of the night.

"Let's go. Get dressed. Hurry up."

The grown-ups had been telling me stories of going to Jerusalem. The land of the Jews, our forefathers, the land of milk and honey. They always said we would go there someday, and now was the time! My mother had just given birth to my little brother, but now she was telling me, "Put your shoes on, we're leaving."

She took me out into the darkness and put me on a horse with my grandmother. I trembled with terror, already missing my friends. But I just had to hold tight to my grandmother and trust the adults that we were going to an even better place than the one we were leaving.

It was 1980. My family and three hundred other members of our village were making aliyah: the journey to Israel that, we believed, every Jew was expected to make in their lifetime. But we were literally walking there, and never returning. The plan had been in the works for months. Following the assassination of Emperor Haile Selassie, a campaign of mass killings, known as the Red Terror, began sweeping the country, and my family decided that now was the time to go. While our village had not been persecuted or seen violence, we were still forbidden to leave Ethiopia. So we had to travel at night, in secret.

Several village families had pooled their money and hired guides to show us back roads out of Ethiopia. We loaded up wagons, horses, and donkeys with sacks filled with flaxseed, teff, coffee, chickpeas, and honey. The night my grandmother pulled me out of bed was no coincidence: There was a full moon that would light our way.

Our three-hundred-person caravan spent the next several weeks traveling mostly at night, trying to evade the authorities and resorting to bribing those we did encounter. But the biggest challenge was simply surviving in the hot, arid desert. We had brought a limited supply of water, and our guides, though knowledgeable, were often mistaken about the locations of rivers and streams. Eventually, this led to desperation. After the last jug ran dry, people began to collapse with thirst. Others frantically dug deep into dry sand with their fingers until they hit enough water for all of us to wet our lips. My aunt says that at one point, I was so thirsty that I told her, "Just bury me here and go, because I don't think I'm going to make it." Thankfully, this was just before a river was sighted in the distance.

We ran into the cool water and drank all that we could. We submerged ourselves in the water and joyfully waded and swam. Then we got back up on the horses and kept moving.

My mother tried to make the journey easier and prepare me for our new home by telling stories of Jerusalem, the land of milk and honey. The one thing we never sacrificed, no matter where we were, was observing the Shabbat. As observant Jews, it was important to us not to skip this even in dangerous circumstances. It was also comforting to know that there would be at least one day a week when we did not have to be on the move. We always did our best to find a safe spot on Fridays so that the women could build a fire and bake kita (page 58), a simple bread. Once sundown came, we spent the day eating the kita and relaxing. It was a relief when we happened upon other Jewish villages, where we could camp and buy food.

After three weeks, we reached the Sudanese border and bribed our way past the border patrol. We reached a village in El Gadarif, home to a number of other Ethiopian refugees, who welcomed us with rented houses, and provided meals. They showed us where we could buy coffee and flour. We were jubilant, thinking that the most dangerous part of the journey was over, and soon we would be in Israel.

Becoming Minorities in Sudan

In reality, it would take another two years for us to leave Sudan. During this time, we never discussed our religion with the local Sudanese people, most of whom were Muslim. There were no public drums beating to signify Shabbat, and certainly no moment when everyone in the community ran down to the river. In Sudan, it was just our family, praying alone in our house. We cooked enough for two days, but did not tell our neighbors why. No one asked each other about their religion: Our personal situation, as well as the political situation around us, was far too unstable to risk this. The most I ever told other kids was "I'm not allowed to eat that."

Still, our Sudanese neighbors were so welcoming. They cooked for me and invited me over to play with their children. Vendors chatted with me and handed me free oranges. I remember the scent of fried dough from other street vendors, as well as peanuts—boiled and roasted—and the most delicious fava beans. Though we were not united by religion, we did begin to lead a life that felt as communal as the one we had left.

I was about six when what looked like a local Sudanese man approached my family. But it was actually my cousin Ferede Aklum (page xxxi), who was now working with the Mossad, Israel's national security agency, to help smuggle Jews into Israel. Though I was too young to understand the details, I'll never forget our jubilation at seeing my cousin, who had been wanted by the Ethiopian government for his work, and who we had feared was dead. Now here he was, alive and helping us get to the mythical city of Jerusalem!

The first time we tried to leave Sudan by Jeep, we were stopped at the border and sent back. Eventually, though, we were smuggled to Khartoum, the capital of Sudan, where we pretended we were going to Saudi Arabia for the pilgrimage to Mecca. In reality, we met two drivers—one Kenyan, one Scottish—and drove south through Uganda and Kenya, where we hoped to catch a plane to Israel. The Scottish guide, Jack, and I became fast friends. He taught me my first words of English, and let me look out the top of the Jeep as we drove through Kenya. I gazed at the towering elephants and the striped zebras. I particularly remember a beautiful, lanky brown-and-white giraffe sprinting away from us, scared at the sound of our motor. The giraffe was so tall!

This part of the journey was free of the desperation we had experienced en route to Sudan. We picked and ate tropical fruit that we encountered along the way: pineapples, mangoes, bananas. We drank a lot of coffee. We were able to buy food from

sympathetic tribes, and once we got to Nairobi, we were thrilled to be able to eat Ethiopian food at a restaurant run by Ethiopians.

Our papers and connections successfully got us onto a commercial flight to Tel Aviv. When we landed, we all kissed the tarmac and wept. Relatives came to hug us, kiss us, dance with us. My grandmother held my hand and kissed me.

We were finally in the Holy Land. The years of effort and sacrifice had paid off.

Minorities Again

Settling into our new home, we quickly realized that our dark skin set us far apart from most Israelis, including other fellow new arrivals at the integration center we moved into. We were probably the only Jews in the world who didn't realize how many white Jews there were—and vice versa! Many of our fellow immigrants who had never seen Black Jews called us names.

Now, instead of practicing our religion in secret, we found ourselves in the exact opposite situation: we had to prove that we were in fact Jewish. The Israeli government insisted that we formally convert to Judaism, which was particularly insulting to us as the people we saw seemed far less observant about traditions that were, to us, nonnegotiable. We had risked our lives on the road to rest on the Shabbat. Here, we were shocked to see people doing chores and driving during that same time. We had never seen Jews observe their traditions this way.

Entering the country, government social workers gave us all new Israeli names—ones that were easier to pronounce and write, like Ilana, Rivka, and Yaffa—selected at random, stripping us of our previous identities.

We also had to face the challenges of preparing Ethiopian food with limited access to ingredients. Making acceptable injera took many months, and finally we found a solution with some improvisation with a nonstick skillet and wheat flour. Thankfully, we could make dabo, as that required only wheat flour. Initially, this bothered the adults much more than it bothered me: I simply could not get enough Israeli food. I loved the crunch of the falafel balls, packed with ground chickpeas and herbs. I watched with awe as children at school unpacked their sandwiches of eggy challah bread slathered with Hashahar Ha'ole sweetened chocolate spread, the most wondrous combination I could have imagined.

Eventually my family moved to Ashkelon, a coastal town, to be near my uncle. Living there opened me to the vast diversity of the Jewish world: We were surrounded not just by Ethiopians but also immigrants from Yemen, Tunisia, and Morocco. While we continued to face prejudice because we were Black, my gregarious personality meant I made friends quickly. I was often invited to sleepovers because people were curious about where I was from. I learned Hebrew quickly enough that I began taking my classes with fluent Israeli students. I learned to speak English in school, too.

I spent a few years steering clear of Ethiopian food as I integrated into Israel: I felt ashamed when my non-Ethiopian friends complained it was too spicy. I preferred schnitzel and loved to eat sabra, the prickly pear that grew on the way to the beach. My mother and the other adults still cooked Ethiopian food, but they often toned down the level of spice and began incorporating ingredients such as bouillon powder and tomato paste that they found in the local grocery stores. They began making lots of roasted chicken, rice, and pasta for us kids.

I still loved Shabbat, the sounds of music and cleaning on Fridays, the smell of fresh challah and other special celebratory dishes. I loved hearing the siren that signified sundown, and I especially loved going to synagogue with Jews from all over the world—Russia, India, Iraq, and England.

I grew up hearing about the kibbutz—the Israeli communal settlement—and its cooperative life on a farm reminded me of my childhood village. I decided to spend four of my teenage years working on one, Kibbutz Alumim, and I loved the process of growing our own vegetables, milking our own cows, using those ingredients to make delicious food, and eating in a communal dining hall. We worshiped in a beautiful synagogue amid fields of carrots and jojoba plants, avocado groves, hundreds of cows, goats, horses, and donkeys, a huge chicken coop, and a swimming pool. I baked dabo, learned about Ashkenazi food, and found that I loved kugel. I made lifelong friends from around the globe, including Tunisia and Great Britain, some of whom came home with me on weekends.

After graduation, I served in the Israeli Defense Forces, which gave me such a boost of confidence that in 1996, I decided to travel through North, Central, and South America. Part of this involved a stop to see New York City—where I fell immediately, unexpectedly, and deeply in love. I marveled at how so many people of so many different ethnicities gave the city such energy, such vibration!

Finding My Calling in Harlem
I returned to Israel for a few years, but I soon realized I was longing to go back to New York. I had been so used to being an ethnic

minority that I was captivated by the Black history on every corner of Harlem, and the thriving Black-owned businesses. I wanted to be part of the evolution of such a beautiful culture. I soon shocked my family by announcing I was moving to New York. I may have had no connections in the city, but I knew I could make them.

And I did. I made friends easily, and started teaching Hebrew. But again, I found that being Black and Jewish was a combination that surprised people. I found myself answering the question "Are you Jewish?" over and over again.

Over the years, I met other Ethiopian Jews and we began talking about the best ways to raise awareness of our small but vibrant community. Eventually, we launched a nonprofit organization, the Beta Israel of North America Cultural Foundation, which helps Ethiopian Jews integrate into New York City society, and seeks a wider audience for our culture through film screenings, speaking engagements, cooking classes, and Shabbat dinners featuring Ethiopian food. Over time, this dialogue brought openness, acceptance, and awareness of the diversity within the Jewish community, particularly regarding Jews of color.

As I continued to be a public advocate for Ethiopian Jewish culture, I realized that food and its significance—our distinct stews and sauces and the meaning behind them—was a missing link in the education we were providing. Harlem's food scene was so lively, so diverse, but it lacked an Ethiopian Jewish standpoint.

I decided that to fully tell my story, I needed to open my own restaurant. I named it Tsion Café, which means "the ultimate spiritual place" in Hebrew, a variation on Israel's Mount Zion. When my husband, Padmore John, and I opened the restaurant, we found an immediately welcoming community eager to eat, drink, and learn. We see so many different ages, races, and cultures, and we answer so many different questions.

Now you too, dear reader, are part of that same community—the one that extends from Ethiopia to Sudan to Israel to Harlem to your home. I welcome you, and I invite you to learn how you can bring the long Beta Israel tradition of hospitality to your own kitchen.

ISRAEL

SUDAN

KHARTOUM

ETHIOPIA

PORTRAIT

ACCEPTING MY INDEPENDENCE
MY MOTHER, AZALECH FEREDE

A portrait of my mother, Azalech Ferede, hangs in my restaurant.
Her brown eyes are wide and wise. She wears Habesha kemis
(Ethiopian dress). In this picture, I can see both the shy and
humble person I knew as well as the head-turning fashionista my
aunties say she was when she was young. Today, her spirit guides

AZALECH'S DISHES

me in everything I do. I still use her spice mixes and so many of her recipes, but most important it was her sense of hospitality—the belief that it is a great honor to feed a weary traveler—that shapes everything I do.

My mother would rise in the early morning to roast coffee from the raw green beans, burning incense and frankincense (an aroma that you can't escape), sharing in the coffee ceremony (see Buna, page 171) with the neighbors. Each Thursday, she would start sifting the flour for dabo, the traditional bread that's part of our Sabbath, which begins on Friday at sundown. My mother made her dabo with milk and honey, like the "promised land" of Israel, a place that was always spoken of with hope. She gave me a small piece of the dough to roll, bake, and later, eat with clarified butter and a cup of hot shahi (spiced tea, page 179).

When I was born, my mother gave me the name of Tevletz; in our native Tigrinya language, it means "to be the most successful and accomplished." So I always knew what she had in mind for me. I started to walk when I was just nine months old, and ever after, she said that I was somebody in a hurry, with many things to do. That proved to be true—sometimes to her dismay. After I served in the military, I packed all my possessions in a backpack and set off to explore the world. "You just got out of the army—maybe you want to spend some time at home?" my mother asked. But she knew and accepted that I traveled to the beat of a different drummer. This was in the days before cell phones and Internet cafés, so I'd send postcards from each of the places I visited. I didn't tell her exactly what I was doing—she really didn't need to know about me bungee jumping in the Amazon or hiking through the jungle in Peru—but one of her great gifts to me was accepting my independence and trusting my judgment, even when it meant that I settled far away from her in New York.

After the birth of my daughter, my mom came to visit. While she couldn't speak the language, she could now see New York's energy and melting pot for herself. She could see why I chose the city—or why the city chose me.

We spoke about the restaurant I wanted to open. The plan was for her to come to New York for several months to help me.

She never arrived. Shortly after her visit, she was diagnosed with leukemia, and she died just a year later. Her death came on December 23, 2015, during a religious fast, and hours after my youngest sister, Hava, gave birth to my nephew, Dor. Hava named Dor in my mother's honor: His name means "he is the generation."

Today her portrait, painted as a gift by my staff, hangs on the wall in the restaurant, inspiring me still.

BETA ISRAEL HISTORY

There have been Ethiopian Jews since antiquity.

There is considerable evidence, from archeologists and scholars, that Ethiopians widely practiced the religion of ancient Israel in pre-Christian times. While experts are divided on how Judaism first came to Ethiopia, Dr. Ephraim Isaac (page 238), the director of the Institute of Semitic Studies in Princeton, told me, "In legend, in history, in language, the history of Ethiopian Jews and their connection to the land of Israel is very firm." Dr. Isaac, who is also the chair of the Board of the Ethiopian Peace and Development Center, added, "Judaism was both the state and the popular religion in Ethiopia until 330."

Some Jewish traditions hold that the introduction of the religion of ancient Israel to Ethiopia happened in the time of Moses. According to a story in the collection of scriptural teachings known as the Midrash Rabbah, Moses fled from Egypt to Ethiopia, where he spent forty years as king. Moses subsequently returned to Egypt and led the exodus of the Israelites from Egypt. The Biblical book of Numbers, verse 13, refers to Moses's Ethiopian wife, which could be a reference to Zipporah or another woman of Ethiopian origin whom he had also married when he was in Ethiopia.

Other theories about how Judaism first came to Ethiopia trace back to the Tribe of Dan making their way to Ethiopia after the fall of the First Temple. This theory was eventually used in the 1970s by Sephardic Chief Rabbi Ovadia Yosef to recognize the religious status of Ethiopian Jews, and to fulfill their birthright to return to Israel.

The story of Makeda, sometimes known as the Queen of Sheba, holds great importance in understanding the history of the Beta Israel. The fourteenth-century book, the Kebra Nagast, the work that is known as the "national epic of Ethiopia," written in Ge'ez (the ancient Ethiopic language), describes Makeda's visit to King Solomon and their ensuing love affair. The work relates how Makeda decided to visit Solomon's court, where she was amazed by his wisdom, and he by her beauty. He made her promise not to touch anything in his house without his explicit permission and he in turn would not touch her. The night before she departed to return home, King Solomon served her salty and spicy food. Makeda became thirsty late at night and drank from a jar of water by the king's bed, thus breaking her promise.

Their eventual union resulted in the birth of their son, Menelik, who was later made the first Emperor of Ethiopia. When asked about his father, Makeda shows him a mirror image of his own face. Menelik returned to Israel and came face-to-face with Solomon. Although Solomon wanted Menelik to succeed him, he insisted that his son return to his mother's country, and asked all the firstborn sons of the leaders of Israel to accompany Menelik, including the son of the High Priest.

The son of the High Priest, regretting that he would not get to officiate in the Temple before the Ark of the Covenant, conspired with Menelik to make a copy of the Ark—and take the original to Ethiopia with them. The land of Israel was darkened and when the Israelites discovered that the original Ark was missing, they pursued Menelik but could not catch him and his entourage. So, to this day, Ethiopians believe that the original Ark is in the Church of Maryam Zion in Axum, the Tigray region of Ethiopia, guarded by a succession of lone monks who live there all their lives.

Another story of great significance in the history of the Beta Israel speaks of an Ethiopian coming to worship in Jerusalem in pre-Christian times. Shortly after the death of Jesus, the Apostles went into various parts of Israel, the Roman world, and other nations. One story in the Book of Acts in the New Testament recounts an Ethiopian eunuch who went to worship in the Temple in Jerusalem. He was returning to Ethiopia when he ran into the apostle Philip. Philip converted the eunuch to Christianity, and in turn the eunuch brought Philip to the court of the throne in Ethiopia.

This story points clearly to the fact that there were Jews in Ethiopia, even before Christian times; that they even used to come to worship in the Temple in Jerusalem and read the Book of the Prophet Isaiah.

Besides such stories, Dr. Isaac notes a number of other ties between Israel and Ethiopia. Ancient Red Sea trade included many Jewish traders. Some of them settled in Yemen, which had come under the rule of Ethiopian rulers in both pre-Christian and Christian times. As Dr. Isaac explained to me, the books of Job and Isaiah mention the trade of spices and gold between Israel and Ethiopia, as well as trade in the Red Sea. Dr. Isaac points out that three of our most important spices—cardamom, coriander, and cumin—are mentioned in the Bible as foods eaten by ancient Israelites.

After 330 CE, the centuries that followed saw differing religions rule Ethiopia. During the rise of the Ethiopian Orthodox Church starting in the fourth century, Beta Israel (including my ancestors) settled in villages in the Tigray and Gondar regions of Ethiopia, experiencing both peaceful times and times of great religious persecution.

The 1970s marked a major turning point in Beta Israel history. After Yosef, the chief Sephardic Rabbi, decreed that the Beta Israel could make aliyah in Israel, my family and thousands of others began planning their journeys, and the eventual mass exodus of Ethiopian Jews to our homeland "was one of the most remarkable events in Jewish history," Dr. Isaac said.

During the 1970s, '80s, and '90s, thousands of families journeyed to Israel on their own, relying on the assistance of an intimate network of Beta Israel individuals as well as the kindness of strangers in a number of countries. While this pipeline delivered Ethiopian Jews to the shores of Israel, advocacy from the Beta Israel community and allies in Europe and the US continued to apply pressure on Israel and Ethiopia to destigmatize the journey and offer support.

This pressure eventually led to three Israeli military operations that helped the Beta Israel resettle: Operations Moses, Joshua, and Solomon saw the arrival of over 100,000 Jews in Israel.

Today, we Beta Israel are much smaller in numbers than the Ashkenazi, Sephardic, or Mizrahi Jews (there are about 160,000 of us in Israel, and fewer than 1,000 in the United States). Our food and traditions are often eclipsed by those of European Jews and their descendants. All of this has led to people frequently asking me if I am really Jewish. The answer, going back millennia, is an emphatic yes.

A REAL-LIFE SUPERHERO
FEREDE AKLUM

My cousin Ferede Aklum is known as the Moses of the Ethiopian Jewish community. He guided hundreds of us out of Ethiopia to Israel under perilous circumstances, often at great risk to himself. He worked closely with the Mossad in Israel, connected with local guides who knew back roads and hidden spots, and raised money to bribe border authorities. His daughter Mali said he did it all with no expectation of recognition, and that the stress of his work most likely shortened his life: He died in 2009, a few months shy of his sixtieth birthday. Like Moses, he wandered through many deserts over his lifetime while leading so many others to the promised land but was never able to truly enjoy it for himself.

Anyone who saw the Netflix movie *The Red Sea Diving Resort* may remember the Ethiopian Jewish agent played by Michael K. Williams who helps the Mossad evacuate Ethiopian Jewish refugees to Israel. This character was based on Ferede, but our family felt it did not give him the credit he deserved. Ferede's legacy was so much more than just as a helper: He shows the resourcefulness of our community to help ourselves.

Ferede, a bright young man from a well-respected family in Tigray (my grandmother and his mother were sisters), trained as a teacher in Addis Ababa, where he earned a commendation from then-emperor Haile Selassie. Eventually, he came back to Tigray to establish a school there. He was formally the headmaster but quickly became the de facto community leader of that region. Whenever someone wanted something done, whether Jewish, Christian, or Muslim, they would come to Ferede for help. This is what first brought him to the attention of the Mossad, and he began working with them to bring Ethiopian Jews to Israel.

This became perilous in 1978 when then-Israeli prime minister Moshe Dayan revealed that Israel was exchanging Ethiopian Jews for weapons. The Ethiopian government then put a target on the back of anyone involved with this plan, and Ferede was quickly identified and hunted by the government. He escaped to Sudan, and sent a telegram to his contacts in Tel Aviv to let them know he had arrived.

The Mossad sent an agent, Danny Limor, to bring Ferede to Israel. But Limor was a stranger to Ferede. And besides, Ferede knew that there were even more people in danger, including his younger brothers, whom the Ethiopian government was trying to force into the military. So he sent them with Limor to Israel. Once he received a picture of them there, he sent it to his mother in Tigray, to show her there was a safe route to Israel. His mother then took her children, nieces, and nephews and fled. All of this paved the way for his mother's sister—my grandmother—to flee with me and the rest of our family.

Once Ferede arrived in Sudan, he ended up passing through the home of Samira, a fellow native of Tigray. At birth, Samira had

been given the name Gaseseche, meaning "blooming, evergreen." Her parents had arranged for her to marry young, but she defied their wishes and in a daring move, fled by herself to Sudan. There she changed her name to Samira.

When she encountered Ferede, Samira quickly recognized that he was Ethiopian, and gave him refuge, allowing him to hide in her house. When the police came looking, she told them she had never seen him. It wasn't until later that Ferede and Samira realized that they were both from Tigray and their grandmothers were best friends. As Ferede continued his activities, more and more Ethiopian Jewish refugees began hiding with Samira. Eventually, Ferede told her what was going on, and she decided to become an operative as well. Their home in Sudan became a sort of underground railroad for Beta Israel fleeing Ethiopia, the centerpiece of the movement to smuggle the Beta Israel into Israel: Anyone who made it across the border knew where the house was, and how to get in touch with Ferede. Samira was helped by her established connections in Sudan and by the fact that no one suspected she was an operative. Samira is even lesser known than Ferede, and gets very little public recognition and acknowledgment. She is one of the countless heroes of the Ethiopian Jewish story, and her name deserves to be right alongside Ferede's as one of the great leaders of the Beta Israel.

Ferede and Samira eventually married and had eight children. I had the honor of interviewing one of them, Mali Aklum.

Mali spent little time with Ferede, but when she did, he was easy to talk to, and freely listened and advised. He was not nearly as strict as many other Ethiopian fathers. He was encouraging, open, and instilled in her a sense of security and independence. That time is something she cherishes and holds dear, although she regrets how little time she was able to spend with him.

Like many Ethiopian children who grew up in Israel, Mali was taught to be very respectful to adults. She was also very shy, and never looked teachers in the eyes. This was often misinterpreted by her Israeli teachers as not understanding the work, and led to them forcing her to repeat first grade.

Mali calls this one of the defining traumas of her life: leaving behind her friends and having to repeat a curriculum that she already knew. When she reached seventh grade, she saw a chance to avenge this. She came to the conclusion that she wanted to go to boarding school, which was considered a big step for any teenager. And not only did she want to go to boarding school, she wanted to skip a grade to make up for what she had lost.

Mali was determined. She did all the paperwork. She got recommendations from her teachers, which they gladly gave. She passed all the tests on her own. And what's more, she showed the national education minister's office proof that she was old enough to be in eighth grade.

As a result, the school called the house and congratulated her on her acceptance. Mali was thrilled. But her mother, Samira, was against the whole plan. Mali was too young to go to boarding school, Samira said; she wanted her to stay home.

But Mali's father, Ferede, took a different stance. When Mali recounted all the work she had done, Ferede told her he was amazed by her persistence, by the amount of thought she had put into the process. In a rare instance of questioning Samira's decisions, he got involved and said, "She went through all of these hurdles, she did it on her own, she deserves to go anywhere she wants."

Ferede Aklum knew what it was like to have ambition, independence, and the ability to follow his own path. And he recognized the same qualities in his daughter. With his support, Mali was off to boarding school.

A Man of Action

While Ferede didn't share much of his work with Mali or her siblings, she could see that her father was always on the run, that he appeared stressed and had nightmares.

Ferede was a man of action. Many people will brag about what they've done, but he was all about just doing it, and doing it quietly, without wanting attention or credit. This meant that he accomplished a lot, but also that his contributions were not always recognized. Mali told me that she feels he gets less recognition than other Ethiopian activists.

I hope this will change over time. Ferede was one of a kind: Only a few are called and chosen to do this incredible job that requires superhero levels of fortitude and leadership.

My last interaction with Ferede was at a 2004 family vegetarian dinner in Addis Ababa. He was an energetic, friendly, fatherly presence who acted as the host, paying for the meal, taking care of everyone. I shared with him that I was thinking of opening an Ethiopian Israeli restaurant in New York City. I wanted to take our cuisine to a global stage.

"Why not?" Ferede said. "You should go for it."

CHAPTER 1

MAKEDA'S KITCHEN

For generations of my family, the following recipes have built the foundation of Beta Israel culture and community. They have been the difference between feeling lost and feeling at home, surrounded by the smells and tastes of Ethiopia, wherever we are in the world. When I make these recipes now, I think of the resourcefulness of those who came before me, struggling to make our food in a new country.

Happily, most of the ingredients are widely available, and I have adapted the recipes to suit modern kitchens. I hope you make them part of your family's traditions, too. I have named this chapter for the queen we know as Makeda, known in other parts of the world as the Queen of Sheba.

OUR HANDS

Hands are by far the most important part of our kitchen. They are the first tool with which we make dough for bread, wash vegetables, milk cows, work the land, and feed ourselves and each other.

Many consider it "primitive" and unclean to eat with your hands or fingers. We Ethiopians believe exactly the opposite: that it's beneficial for the digestive system to absorb the various minerals and oils from your hands, and that eating with utensils creates a distance between your food and your body. And we mark weddings and other important occasions in our lives with the ritual Gursha: feeding each other mouthfuls of food.

We also emphasize the cleanliness of our hands, meticulously washing them before and after eating and feeding others. In my family, we have a tradition of putting a young child in charge of bringing over a bucket or tray of water, and washing the hands of guests and parents. And we eat injera only with the right hand, to symbolize cleanliness, purity, and closeness to the heart.

We sit around the mesob—a communal basket used as a table—and feed one another, and enjoy each other's company. These are traditions that are not only near and dear to my heart, but are also practiced by many Ethiopians, Africans, and Indigenous people throughout the world.

PANTRY

Teff / Taff

In its raw form, teff is a tiny brown seed packed with a lot of iron, fiber, and protein. When milled into flour, fermented, and used to make bread or porridge, it lends a delicious nutty flavor and tartness. Ethiopia still grows the vast majority of the world's teff, but because it's a nutritious ancient grain, it's becoming more and more common in the United States to see teff flour and pasta in grocery stores. Teff is naturally gluten-free but is often mixed with wheat in baked goods.

Korarima

The secret ingredient in many of my recipes is this nutty, herbal spice that is like an Ethiopian version of cardamom. It tends to come in the form of small black seeds that you should roast (Ground Roasted Korarima, page 26) and then grind in a spice mill or with a mortar and pestle. Just a little is enough to add a unique dimension to your food. It can be purchased at specialty spice shops or online.

Green Cardamom

Ground green cardamom can be substituted for korarima, and is often easier to find at spice shops and grocery stores. The intensely flavored pods are also commonly used in Arabic, Indian, and Scandinavian cooking. Note that this is not the same as black cardamom, which I do not use in my cooking.

Besobela / Tulsi / Ethiopian Basil

This purple basil grows wild in Ethiopia and is a key ingredient in my Mitmita / Dukus / Ethiopian Seasoning Salt (page 12). While regular basil can be substituted, try to source this online or at a spice shop. Its distinctive fruity flavor makes the mitmita truly pop with flavor.

Nug / Niger Seeds

These tiny black seeds have the ability to transport me back in time to my childhood in Ethiopia and my journey to Sudan. Because niger seeds are so nutritious and portable, we relied heavily on them during our travels, and we often nibbled on them for Passover. Some cultures package these as birdseed, but their dark, earthy flavor is an essential part of the Beta Israel diet.

BERBERE

Aromatic Ethiopian Spice Blend

Makes about 2½ cups

This flavorful, aromatic seasoning blend says a lot about the cook who mixes it. I regard this spice mixture less as a formula and more as a way to express myself. I start mine with plenty of dried chili pepper, as is traditional, but then I add a healthy dose of korarima, because I love the nutty, herbal notes it adds. My mother's berbere was heavy on serrano pepper, basil, and tiny nigella seeds, infusing her cooking with a signature spicy bite. While I welcome the growing number of grocery stores that carry berbere in the spice section, I find that many of them overdo it on the paprika and cumin, giving food a much flatter taste. Feel free to use my recipe as a starting point for yours, adding more of any flavors you want to emphasize, while decreasing or omitting any you may dislike. This formula will make enough for a batch of Kulet (page 6), with a little left over.

- 1 cup paprika
- ½ cup cayenne pepper
- 3 tablespoons Ground Roasted Korarima (page 26) or ground cardamom
- 2 tablespoons ground ginger
- 1 tablespoon onion powder
- 1 tablespoon ground coriander
- 1 tablespoon ground cumin
- 1 tablespoon black pepper
- 2 tablespoons fine sea salt
- 1½ teaspoons ground cloves
- 1½ teaspoons ground cinnamon
- 1½ teaspoons ground nutmeg
- 1½ teaspoons ground fenugreek

IN A SMALL BOWL, mix all the ingredients together and transfer to an airtight jar.

Storage Store at room temperature for up to 6 months.

KULET / SILSI

Fragrant Ethiopian Stew Base

Makes about 16 cups

The foundation of all thick, spicy Ethiopian stews starts with slow-cooking onions, garlic, ginger, and berbere until they melt into one another. Let this crimson-colored base bubble for a few hours, and you can have dinner all week. Use it to make chicken stew, fish stew, red lentil stew, or all of them at once. Feel free to halve or double the recipe, too. Ethiopian cooks typically chop the onions finely by hand. I make good use of the food processor to shorten this task, with the same luscious results.

10–12	large yellow onions, peeled and quartered
6	cups vegetable oil, plus more if necessary
2	cups Berbere (page 6)
4	teaspoons minced garlic
2	teaspoons minced fresh ginger
3	tablespoons fine sea salt
8	cups hot water
6	ounces tomato paste (or 12 ounces, if you prefer less heat)
1	tablespoon Ground Roasted Korarima (page 26) or ground cardamom

IN A FOOD PROCESSOR, puree the onions until smooth.

Pour the onions into a large pot and bring to simmer over high heat. Cook, stirring occasionally and reducing the heat if the onions begin browning, until most of the water has evaporated, 35 to 40 minutes.

Stir in the oil and simmer for about 5 minutes to incorporate. Stir in the berbere, garlic, ginger, and salt. The mixture should be moist; if it appears dry, add more hot water, about ½ cup at a time. Cover the pot and cook over medium heat until the onions have taken on a red hue, for another 10 to 15 minutes.

Add the hot water and tomato paste and stir well. Bring to a simmer, then reduce the heat and cook uncovered, stirring occasionally, until the flavors blend and the stew base becomes fragrant, about 1 hour.

Remove from the heat and stir in the korarima. Let cool.

Storage Store in an airtight container in the refrigerator for up to 2 weeks, or in the freezer for up to 3 months.

PORTRAIT

VERED GERMAY
Clinging Tight to Her Faith

My cousin Vered Germay spent some of the most formative years of her life on the journey out of Ethiopia to Sudan, and eventually to Israel. Years that tried and tested her commitment to her faith and her family.

    After arriving in Sudan, to await the journey to Israel, in her early twenties, Vered needed to support herself, and quickly found work as a housekeeper for a wealthy Muslim woman. Her new boss soon realized that Vered was a hard worker and a resourceful person, and she treated Vered with much generosity, constantly sending her home with food for her family. Vered gratefully accepted the sugar, salt, and spices, but one of her boss's regular offerings was camel meat, as she had assumed that Vered was a fellow Muslim. Instead of setting her straight, Vered accepted the meat, left the house, and surreptitiously deposited it in the garbage. She feared for her safety, and her job security, if the woman realized she was Jewish.

Eventually, Vered's boss grew to love her so much that she tried to set up Vered with her own brother. Vered could not agree to marry a Muslim, but worried for her safety. Her family decided that the only solution was for her to be married—and quickly. They set her up with an older Beta Israel man who was also awaiting passage to Israel. This allowed Vered to inform her boss that she was already engaged. While she was sad to lose Vered as an employee, she cared so much about her that she threw Vered an engagement party, where she treated her to beautifully henna-painted hands, and massages with oils and perfumes.

Although Vered's marriage began out of necessity, it blossomed, and soon the couple was expecting their first child. Unfortunately, their daughter arrived when they were still living in Sudan, with no access to medical care. The birth went dreadfully wrong. After hours of labor, the baby had not yet come. No painkillers were available. To save the baby, the lone midwife available sharpened a knife, sterilized it in the fire, and slit open Vered's stomach to retrieve the child. She then stitched the stomach together while Vered screamed in pain alongside her baby's cries.

Both Vered and her child recovered from that traumatic birth. What kept Vered going was the prophecy, in prayers and letters from Ferede Aklum, that "everyone [was] going to make it to the promised land." And three months after her daughter's birth, Vered and her husband got the news that their paperwork to Israel had been finalized.

Well after darkness fell one rainy night, the new mother and her husband and baby got into a car, part of a caravan of Beta Israel families. Their cars stalled in the mud, but eventually they arrived at a nearby port. An Israeli naval ship was waiting to whisk them away but, as Vered recalls, the ship was prohibited from entering Sudanese territory. As a result, it floated miles offshore.

The families instead faced a row of rescue boats made of rubber. Military officers helped them aboard and sailed them into the darkness. Vered is still haunted by the memory of her small boat being lifted high in the sky by a machine, to reach the larger ship.

There, her journey eased. She found herself surrounded by fellow Ethiopians. Doctors. Nurses. They offered her food and medical assistance. Their welcoming words felt healing. "It was like the promised land, already," she says. She still believes that her arrival in Israel was thanks to the prayers of her holy ancestors. "We are in a land of milk and honey, even though it's not perfect," she said. "But this is my land."

One of my favorite examples of how we Beta Israel have adapted to cooking our food in unfamiliar areas is delleh, a deep red paste that can be substituted in an equal amount with berbere in many dishes. Making berbere and delleh is fundamental to Ethiopian food, but it has not always been as simple as stirring up a few spices.

Where Vered and I grew up, it was a time-honored tradition to make delleh from peppers grown on our own farm. The entire community helped with the task and celebrated it. But once we moved to Israel, we had to figure out how to work this activity into urban and suburban areas filled with white Israelis who did not always appreciate the smells of our food. I remember that when my mother roasted her spices, the smell lingered in the kitchens for weeks, as did the smell of fermenting injera. This was no small matter: My relatives remember that many Israelis made it clear that they hated the smell of our spices so much that they would leave apartment buildings because Ethiopian Jews moved into them.

I am so proud of my relatives for not abandoning this food altogether. They knew that it was delicious, beautiful, and healthy. They knew that it was a big part of their culture. They held tight to their traditions. Vered did this by organizing a number of girlfriends who together purchased large amounts of spices, and set days to travel to a forest, park, or another open area. There, they would build a fire, and roast and grind all the spices at once. They made enormous batches that many families could store in the refrigerator or freezer.

Eventually, businesses popped up that would roast and grind spices to our family's specifications—allowing us to make our cherished food while keeping the peace with our new neighbors. And today, I am so proud to pass on these traditions that Vered and others worked so hard to protect.

DELLEH

Ethiopian Berbere Paste

Makes about 1 cup

This deep red paste—which can be substituted in an equal amount for berbere in many dishes—has a big advantage: because the spices are already dissolved, the flavors meld faster and much more smoothly into your food. I've added extra korarima to this recipe, giving it a more floral quality than my berbere itself. Its texture is like that of a more concentrated version of harissa, the Moroccan spice paste.

½ cup Berbere (page 5)
1 teaspoon Ground Roasted Korarima (page 26)
1 teaspoon fine sea salt
⅓ cup olive oil

IN A SMALL BOWL, mix the berbere, korarima, and salt. Add ⅓ cup water and mix. Add the olive oil and mix until well combined.

Storage Store in an airtight container in the refrigerator for up to 6 months. It can also be frozen for up to 1 year.

MITMITA / DUKUS

Ethiopian Seasoning Salt

Makes about 1¾ cups

Once you've tried this unique blend of flavors on meat, you won't go back to a packaged seasoned salt: The deep flavor of mitmita enhances any stew and is ideal for Kitfo (page 155).

—————————

IN A SPICE BLENDER, blend everything until finely ground. Transfer to an airtight jar.

Storage Store at room temperature for 6 months.

½ cup whole dried red chilies

¼ cup dried minced garlic

¼ cup dried minced onion

¼ cup ground ginger

¼ cup unroasted korarima seeds

¼ cup dried besobela (Ethiopian basil) or dried regular basil

2 tablespoons fine sea salt

1 teaspoon ground turmeric

NITER KIBBEH / *TESMI*

Spice-Infused Ethiopian Clarified Butter

Makes about 3 cups

Add spices to butter, simmer until the butter turns a deep mahogany, and you have yourself a staple of Ethiopian cooking that will last in the refrigerator for months. (The recipe can also easily be halved.) This butter lends so many Ethiopian dishes their distinctive flavor. It's worth going the extra mile to find besobela (Ethiopian basil): It's available online, and its delicate floral flavor, combined with the korarima, is one of the many things that sets our food apart. But dried basil can be substituted in a pinch. Use niter kibbeh to sauté meat, swap for oil in stew recipes, drizzle over vegetables or meat, or add a fragrant touch to a bowl of Ethiopian cheese (see Ayib, page 18).

2 pounds (8 sticks) unsalted butter

½ yellow onion, chopped

4 teaspoons minced garlic

2 teaspoons minced fresh ginger

1 tablespoon dried besobela (Ethiopian basil) or dried regular basil

1 tablespoon Ground Roasted Korarima (page 26) or ground cardamom

1 tablespoon ground turmeric

1 teaspoon ground fenugreek or fenugreek seeds

1 teaspoon green cardamom pods

4 whole cloves

3 sprigs fresh thyme, or ½ teaspoon dried thyme

IN A MEDIUM SAUCEPAN, melt the butter over medium-low heat.

Add the onion, garlic, ginger, besobela, korarima, turmeric, fenugreek, cardamom pods, cloves, and thyme. Simmer until the butter foams, about 15 minutes.

Stir the foam down and simmer until the butter becomes brown, clear, and fragrant, 5 to 10 minutes.

Cool to room temperature. Strain the butter through a fine-mesh strainer or cheesecloth, pressing the solids against the strainer to extract all the flavors. Discard the solids.

Storage Store in a jar in the refrigerator for up to 6 months or in the freezer for up to 1 year.

AYIB / AJIBO

Fresh Ethiopian Cheese

Makes about 1 pound

2 quarts whole milk

1 cup distilled white vinegar

Optional for serving: Niter Kibbeh (page 15), Berbere (page 5)

Why make fresh cheese yourself? Because it's easier than you might expect, and its pure milky flavor provides a soothing, cooling counterbalance to spicy stews. In Ethiopian culture, ayib occupies a similar role to that of Indian raita or Greek tzatziki. I often use it as a garnish, and I love to crumble a little on a bite of food before placing it into someone's mouth. But I also like to eat it by itself, topped with a drizzle of Niter Kibbeh (page 15) and a dash of Berbere (page 5).

IN A MEDIUM POT, warm the milk over low heat, stirring occasionally. Bring to a gentle simmer, then slowly swirl in the vinegar, stirring constantly, until fully incorporated.

Leave the pot over low heat as curds begin to form and collect in the middle of the pot.

Meanwhile, set a fine-mesh strainer over a large bowl and line the strainer with cheesecloth, if desired.

When the milk has formed a solid white mass in the center of the pot, after about 10 minutes, immediately strain. Do not press the cheese against the strainer. Keep the strainer over the bowl for another 5 to 10 minutes, until it stops dripping. Use a fork to crumble the cheese into small curds in the strainer.

Serve garnished with the niter kibbeh and/or a sprinkle of berbere, if desired.

Storage Store in the refrigerator for up to 1 week.

HILBE / *ABISH*

Fenugreek Sauce

Makes about ½ cup

This fenugreek sauce is meant to be eaten with Yemenite Chicken Soup (page 159). This is one of several recipes that celebrate the ties between Ethiopians and Yemenites, who often supported and married each other. This recipe is adapted from one given to me by Dr. Ephraim Isaac (page 238), whose remarkable journey led to his becoming one of the world's most prominent Jewish leaders and scholars—starting from his birth in Ethiopia. His Yemenite father had come to a remote part of Ethiopia as a rabbi for a Yemenite community but was kidnapped and held by a remote tribe. After many years, he married the tribal leader's daughter, who converted to Judaism, and they raised seven children, the fifth of whom was Dr. Isaac. The couple observed the Sabbath—Dr. Isaac recalls that his mother always said the weekly blessings over wine, and that they celebrated Jewish holidays.

3 tablespoons ground fenugreek
2 teaspoons Zhoug (page 25)
2 teaspoons fresh lemon juice
1 teaspoon fine sea salt

IN A MEDIUM BOWL, mix the fenugreek and ½ cup water. Cover and let sit at room temperature until it forms a gelatinous paste, at least 1 hour and up to overnight.

The next day, transfer the paste to a food processor. Add ½ cup water, the zhoug, lemon juice, and salt and blend until well combined. Transfer to an airtight container.

Storage Store in the refrigerator for up to 1 week.

HAWAIJ
Warming Yemenite Spice Mix

Makes about 1 cup

I crafted this spice mix inspired by Dr. Ephraim Isaac's Yemenite Chicken Soup (page 159). This version has no salt, giving you more flexibility in the seasoning of your soups. It also makes an excellent rub for meats.

WARM A MEDIUM NONSTICK PAN over medium heat. Add the peppercorns, cumin seeds, coriander seeds, cardamom pods, caraway seeds, and cloves and toast, constantly mixing, until the seeds darken, become fragrant, and begin to pop, 2 to 3 minutes. Immediately transfer to a plate to cool for about 5 minutes.

Pour the peppercorn mixture into a spice grinder. Add the turmeric and cinnamon. Grind into a fine powder (in batches, if necessary). Transfer to an airtight container.

Storage Store at room temperature for up to 1 year.

⅓ cup black peppercorns

⅓ cup cumin seeds

1 tablespoon coriander seeds

1 heaping tablespoon green cardamom pods

1 teaspoon caraway seeds

1 teaspoon whole cloves

2 tablespoons ground turmeric

1 tablespoon ground cinnamon

ZHOUG

Spicy Green Sauce

Makes about 1½ cups

This spicy green herb-filled mixture originated in Yemen and has recently become popular in the United States and the Middle East.

WARM A SMALL SKILLET over medium heat. Add the cumin seeds, coriander seeds, cardamom seeds, and peppercorns and toast until dark and fragrant, 1 to 2 minutes. Transfer to a plate and set aside to cool slightly.

In a food processor, combine the toasted seeds and peppercorns, the cilantro, parsley, serranos, garlic, ginger, lemon juice, olive oil, and salt. Process until emulsified, about 1 minute. Transfer to an airtight container.

Storage Store in the refrigerator for up to 1 week.

- 1 teaspoon cumin seeds
- 1 teaspoon coriander seeds
- 1 teaspoon green cardamom seeds
- 1 teaspoon black peppercorns
- ½ bunch cilantro, leaves and stems, roughly chopped
- ½ bunch flat-leaf parsley leaves, roughly chopped
- 6 serrano peppers, trimmed and roughly chopped
- 8 garlic cloves, peeled but whole
- 2″ piece fresh ginger, peeled and roughly chopped
- ¼ cup fresh lemon juice
- ¼ cup olive oil
- 1 teaspoon fine sea salt

SPICY ZHOUG BUTTER

Makes about ½ cup

I developed this compound butter to gild Ethiopian Barbecue Corn Bread (page 200), but try it on your morning toast or any of my breads.

- 8 tablespoons (4 ounces) unsalted butter, at room temperature
- 3 tablespoons Zhoug (page 25)

IN A STAND MIXER fitted with the paddle, mix the butter and zhoug until well combined, about 1 minute. Serve at room temperature.

Storage Wrap well in plastic wrap and store in the refrigerator for up to 5 days, or in the freezer for up to 1 month.

GROUND ROASTED KORARIMA

Makes about ¼ cup

Korarima—an Ethiopian spice related to cardamom—is a defining flavor in my food: Its complex, nutty, floral quality perks up so many dishes. When you first purchase korarima, it will most likely come in little seeds that you need to grind into a powder to use in my recipes. Here is how I get the most flavor out of these tiny seeds. You can use as many or as few seeds as you have; vary the pan size accordingly.

About ⅓ cup korarima seeds

WARM A MEDIUM NONSTICK PAN over medium heat. Add the korarima seeds and roast until shiny and fragrant, 2 to 3 minutes. Transfer to a plate or bowl and let cool completely.

Transfer to a mortar and pestle or spice grinder and grind into a powder. Transfer to an airtight container.

Storage Store at room temperature for up to 3 months.

CH'EW KEMEM

Earthy Seasoned Salt

Makes about 3 tablespoons

I adapted this salt from a recipe used by my cousin Avejo Aklum (page 101) because I wanted to use it in her Dabo recipe (page 53). I soon found myself using it to flavor other breads, too.

IN A SMALL BOWL, mix together the coriander, salt, niger seeds, fenugreek seeds, and green cardamom seeds. For best results, use immediately.

Storage Store in an airtight container for up to 3 months.

2 tablespoons ground coriander

1 teaspoon fine sea salt

1 teaspoon ground toasted niger seeds

½ teaspoon ground toasted fenugreek seeds

½ teaspoon ground toasted green cardamom seeds

SUFF BASE

Sunflower Seed Base

Makes about 5 cups

Sunflower seeds appear in so many of my Ethiopian food memories. We snacked on them on our journey from Ethiopia to Sudan, sprinkled them on salads, and soaked them for salad dressings and drinks. Not only are they extremely nutritious, their flavor is very close to that of tahini, making them an excellent swap for those who are sensitive to sesame. I created this base to use in the Suff Drink (page 183), Suff Dressing (page 29), and Crunchy Sunflower Cabbage Slaw (page 93).

2 cups sunflower seeds
1 teaspoon fine sea salt

IN A MEDIUM POT, combine the seeds and salt and cover with water. Bring to a boil over medium heat and cook, adding more water as needed to keep the seeds covered, until soft, about 35 minutes.

Drain and rinse well several times. Transfer the seeds to a blender and add 2 cups water. Blend until thick. Drain the mixture in a fine-mesh strainer, pressing on the solids. Discard the solids (they make great garden compost).

Transfer the liquid to a large bowl and mix with 1 cup water. You should have a watery, light-gray liquid. Transfer to an airtight container.

Storage Store in the refrigerator for up to 1 week.

SUFF DRESSING

Sunflower Seed Salad Dressing

Makes about 1⅓ cups

When mixed with vinegar, citrus, and oil, the sunflower base makes a bright, nutty, earthy dressing.

IN A MEDIUM BOWL, whisk together the suff base, oil, lime juice, vinegar, berbere, sugar, and garlic powder.

Storage Store in an airtight container in the refrigerator for up to 1 week.

Note When using this as a salad dressing, serve with lime wedges for squeezing on top.

½ cup Suff Base (page 28)

¼ cup vegetable oil

¼ cup fresh lime juice (from 2 limes)

3 tablespoons apple cider vinegar

½ teaspoon Berbere (page 5)

½ teaspoon sugar

¼ teaspoon garlic powder

SENAFICH

Homemade Mustard

Makes about 1 cup

If you've never made mustard from scratch, I think you'll be pleased with the strength of this one. Ethiopian mustard generally has a more pourable texture than Western mustard, making it good for drizzling or dipping. As this sits in your refrigerator, you'll find the flavor deepens over time.

½ cup mustard powder, whisked or sifted to remove any lumps

⅛ teaspoon fine sea salt

⅛ teaspoon black pepper

1 cup hot water, plus more if necessary

PLACE THE MUSTARD POWDER, salt, and pepper in a large bowl. Slowly whisk in the hot water to give a pourable texture. Pour into an airtight jar and refrigerate for at least 1 day before using.

Storage Store in the refrigerator for up to 2 months.

AWAZE / YE KARAY DELLEH

Tsion Café's Green Hot Sauce

Makes about 2½ cups

The signature hot sauce at my restaurant, Tsion Café, is this refreshing mixture of jalapeños, ginger, and cilantro. Use it to perk up any food: Dollop it on eggs in the morning, serve it with leftover rice, use it to marinate chicken or fish before cooking, or just spoon it on top of any cooked protein. I love it on Kategna (page 50).

IN A FOOD PROCESSOR, pulse the jalapeños, onion, garlic, ginger, cilantro, salt, and black pepper until a chunky sauce forms. Add the lemon juice and 1 tablespoon cold water and process until smooth. Add the olive oil and pulse until incorporated. Transfer to an airtight container.

Storage Store in the refrigerator for up to 3 months.

6–8 jalapeño peppers, roughly sliced into rounds

1 yellow onion, peeled and quartered

10 garlic cloves, peeled but whole

1" slice fresh ginger, peeled and cut into a few pieces

½ bunch fresh cilantro, leaves and thin stems, roughly chopped

¾ teaspoon fine sea salt

¼ teaspoon black pepper

1 tablespoon fresh lemon juice

1 tablespoon olive oil

ETHIOPIAN COFFEE EXTRACT

Makes about ½ cup

Coffee extract delivers a shot of concentrated coffee flavor to my honey cake (see Ma'arn Tzava Cake, page 205) and Kaffa Martini (page 193) and is delicious in iced coffee drinks. While you can buy coffee extract, I recommend making your own.

½ cup dark rum

½ cup whole Ethiopian light roast coffee beans

COMBINE THE RUM AND COFFEE in a glass jar with a tight-fitting lid. Store at room temperature for at least 1 week before using. Shake the jar periodically to combine the flavors. Strain out the coffee beans before using.

Storage Store at room temperature for up to 1 year.

CHAPTER 2

BREAD

For us, bread is where it all begins. It's the centerpiece of Shabbat and the foundation of the Ethiopian dinner table. It has always been a point of pride in my family, whether we were making it from scratch in Ethiopia or adapting to new flours in Israel.

My aunt Rishan Mesele (page 44) told me that on our family farm in Ethiopia, making bread was done from the raw teff grain, which first had to be cleaned of rocks and sand. Then she took the grain to a big rock, sifted it carefully and then roasted the flour on the mogogo—a big ceramic skillet used to make injera. Rishan mixed the ground grain with water to make a batter, and let it sit for a day or two to let it rise, before spreading it out on the mogogo.

Lucky for you and me, the process of making bread no longer requires such labor. This chapter details how you can make bread that tastes similar to what my family made in Ethiopia, no special cooking equipment necessary.

INJERA / TAITA

Ethiopian Flatbread

Makes eight to ten 10-inch injera

Injera, the famed Ethiopian bread, has many uses beyond just as a delicious, nutritious flatbread. It can be an edible plate, covered with stews. It can be a utensil—tear off a piece and use it to scoop up meat or vegetables with your hands. Injera is usually made with a teff sourdough starter—the one we use at Tsion Café is six years old and is fed every day to keep up with our hungry customers. I've developed this recipe for home cooks who have no starter. By using yeast, you can make injera in as little as 3 days. It can be a complex process, and one that takes practice to get right—but the payoff is that signature tangy flavor and light texture. And because this recipe is made entirely with teff flour, it is naturally gluten-free (if you use gluten-free yeast and baking powder).

2 cups (460 grams) ivory teff flour

2 cups (460 grams) brown teff flour

½ teaspoon active dry yeast

5 cups (1,200 grams) lukewarm water, plus more if necessary

Pinch of baking powder

DAY 1

In a large container with a tight-fitting lid, use your hands to combine both teff flours and the yeast. Add 3 cups of the lukewarm water and aggressively mix with your hands until a thick batter forms with no dry lumps of flour. Pour the remaining 2 cups lukewarm water around the sides of the bowl and mix with your hands until a thick batter forms; it may be chunky.

Cover the container and let it ferment in the warmest room of your house for about 24 hours. Do not place outdoors, in direct sunlight, or on top of a radiator or heater, or the batter may dry out.

DAY 2

Uncover the container: The water and flour will have begun to separate. Pour off any water on the top. If the mixture still has lumps of flour, use your hands to break them up, adding up to ½ cup more lukewarm water if necessary to blend. Mix the batter until smooth. Cover the container and ferment for another 24 hours in a warm spot.

Injera continues

DAY 3

Uncover the container: The mixture should be mostly cohesive. Pour off any water on the top. Add the baking powder and mix with your hands or a whisk to form a smooth, pourable batter (similar to pancake or crepe batter). If the batter is too thick to pour, add ¼ cup lukewarm water and whisk well.

TO COOK

Warm a 12-inch nonstick pan over high heat, then reduce the heat to medium.

Pour about ¾ cup of batter into the center of the pan and quickly swirl to coat the entire pan. Cover the pan and cook until small bubbles form over the entire surface of the batter, the edges become dry, and no whiteness remains on the surface, about 45 seconds.

Slide a wide spatula under the injera and carefully lift it off the pan. It should be spongy, covered with holes on top, and not browned on the bottom. (If it is browned, reduce the heat for the next injera.)

Repeat with the rest of the batter. Wrap injera individually in plastic wrap, stack in a zip-top plastic bag, and refrigerate for up to 1 week, or freeze for up to 1 month.

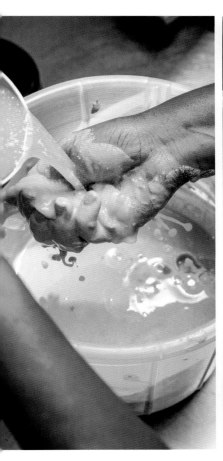

DIRKOSSH / *KOROSHO*

Injera Chips

Serves about 4

The Ethiopian answer to pita chips, with injera's signature tang in each crunchy bite. Simply slice any leftover injera, place it in the oven—no oil or frying needed!—and dip into Hummus with Spicy Silsi (page 137) or your favorite dip. I like to make these large, the better for scooping: they curl as they toast up.

2 Injera (page 37)

PREHEAT THE OVEN to 350°F. Place an ovenproof rack over a large sheet pan.

Trim the ragged edges off the injera. Cut the injera into rectangle or diamond shapes about 1 inch by 2 inches.

Place the injera in a single layer on the prepared rack and sheet pan. Bake on the middle rack of the oven until crunchy, 10 to 15 minutes, depending on the thickness of the injera. Let cool before storing.

Storage Store in an airtight container at room temperature for up to 2 months.

RISHAN MESELE

"I Risked My Life for My Judaism"

My aunt Rishan Mesele's first name means "skyscraper, above all else," and she has truly earned it. From a very early age, Rishan was forced to carry an entire household's worth of responsibilities on her shoulders.

Rishan was born in 1965 in a village called Adigrat. Her father, Woundemagnyo Mesele, moved his family to a village called Erar, but he passed away when Rishan was four. It fell to Rishan to help her mother look after her six siblings, particularly her youngest brother, and to help in the kitchen.

When Rishan was nine, her mother, Einalem Deit, fell ill and passed away. From that moment, Rishan's childhood ended, and she had to learn to function as an adult. She had to make the family's food from scratch, using what her mother had already taught her, as well as a lot of trial and error. She had to carry water from the river to the family home. She had to take care of her youngest brother, and mind the family's sheep. She missed her parents, she missed being a child, but she had no choice but to act as the head of the household.

In retrospect, she says that while this was immeasurably hard, it also taught her valuable resilience and improvisation skills that were crucial on her harrowing journey to Israel—and later in figuring out how to cook Ethiopian food in her new country.

Like many of us, Rishan, then sixteen, left Ethiopia in the middle of the night. When the sun fell on Friday night, the village had already packed up their water, food, and supplies. After marking the Shabbat, Rishan and her fellow travelers started out on Saturday night, and spent the next month and a half walking.

They first stopped in a place called Mezega, which had become a sort of central stop for groups journeying to Israel from different Ethiopian villages. Rishan's village group stayed there for more than a week, linking up with other groups and obtaining guides and dogs who could help them navigate the desert on their way to Sudan. It was also an auspicious stop for Rishan, who met a woman who would later become her mother-in-law.

Now traveling in a larger group, Rishan had to navigate an area with a dearth of water sources, which became particularly trying during the Sabbath. One Friday afternoon, with sundown approaching, the group began looking for rivers or streams. As darkness fell, the young men got on horses and rode until they found an area that looked wet. They started digging and were eventually able to fill their pitchers and take them back to the group, who thought Shabbat was settled. They could now prepare kicha and vegetables and rest for Shabbat.

However, the water unexpectedly ran out the next morning, leaving the group of devout Beta Israel in a quandary: whether to work on Shabbat. Many pointed out that it was forbidden by the Torah. Others argued that they should search for water, otherwise they might die. The disagreements continued until Shabbat ended, and they loaded their horses and continued on their journey, walking all night without water. Some people fainted. Rishan remembers overwhelming thirst.

RISHAN'S DISHES

Finally, more than thirty-six hours later, the group arrived at the Bahr as-Salam river, which they would have to cross in order to reach Sudan. In relief, they drank, made food, took a break from walking, and rested. But one of the most dangerous parts of their journey was about to begin. They were confronted by Sudanese soldiers who demanded that they hand over their weapons. Finally, they did, and the soldiers let them cross the river.

Once they entered Sudan, many things got easier, particularly getting water: The group settled near a small river, alongside other Jewish families who had pitched tents.

After six months, the Mossad helped Rishan's group journey to the Sudanese capital, Khartoum. They then flew to France, where they spent one night at a guesthouse (where, Rishan recalls, they did not recognize any food except for bread) and saw snow for the first time. Then they boarded an airplane and were flown to Israel.

At the airport, Rishan and her fellow travelers kissed the ground in gratitude. They were immediately taken to process paperwork, and without any ceremony or meaning, the Israeli government gave Rishan a new name: Rivka.

"They didn't even put my name in parentheses. From that moment I was just Rivka to the Israelis," Rishan said. But to her close family and friends from Ethiopia, "I always stayed Rishan."

When government officials led her to a mikvah, at first she did not understand that this was a Jewish "conversion" ceremony that was being held because the Israeli government did not believe she was Jewish. When she realized the truth, Rishan felt as if she had been punched. "I walked here. I risked my life for my Judaism," Rishan said. "I know who I am, and I am Jewish. I have always been and will always remain Jewish. A mikvah, it's just water."

After the registration, she stayed at a government-run absorption center for new immigrants for a few weeks until her brother-in-law came from Ashkelon and asked Rishan to come stay with him. Rishan attended an Ulpan, a language institute, to learn Hebrew. Her teachers were impressed and wanted to send her to a boarding school, but she needed to work to support her family. So she and her half sister Asefash Mesele (page 148) went to work in a factory. She then briefly worked at the menswear company Polgat before meeting her husband, Arghey, whose mother she had met in Mizga during her journey. Today, the couple are the parents of six children and have one granddaughter.

CORN and WHEAT INJERA

Ethiopian Flatbread for a Move to Israel

Makes 8 to 10 injera

When most of our families moved to Israel, they had trouble making bread. They could make injera quickly in the warm climate of Ethiopia, where teff flour was easily accessible. But in Israel, teff flour was nowhere to be found, and the cooler climate meant that the bread took longer to make—sometimes up to four times as long, recalls my aunt Rishan Mesele (page 44).

So the Beta Israel community got to work figuring out how to make injera from corn and wheat, the two most accessible alternatives to teff. My aunt noted that corn became important to those who quickly tired of the blander white flours. The women couldn't locate pans to make large injera, so they began making individual portions in smaller pans.

I developed this recipe based on Rishan's recollections, and I was so excited to see the bright, sunny color that meant that my family had successfully brought a bit of Ethiopia to Israel.

- 4 cups (520 grams) self-rising flour
- 1 cup (100 grams) fine corn flour
- ½ teaspoon active dry yeast
- 4¼ cups (1,020 grams) warm water
- 1 teaspoon baking powder

DAY 1

In a tall, narrow container with a lid, mix the self-rising flour, corn flour, yeast, and 4 cups of the warm water. Pour the remaining ¼ cup warm water over the surface of the batter, cover, and let sit at room temperature for 24 hours.

DAY 2

After 24 hours, the batter should have some scattered bubbles on the surface. Cover and continue fermenting for another 24 hours.

DAY 3

After 48 hours, a low to moderate concentration of bubbles should cover the surface. A clear brown/grayish liquid will appear on top, which is an indicator that the batter has begun fermenting. The scent should be slightly sour and will have a hint of acetone. Whisk in ½ cup warm water, then continue whisking rapidly for a few minutes to aerate the batter. Let sit overnight.

Corn and Wheat Injera continues

DAY 4

The mixture should be light and bubbly (if not, it may need more fermentation time). Whisk the baking powder into the batter. Warm an 8- or 9-inch nonstick pan over medium-high heat. Pour ½ cup batter into the pan and rotate the pan so that the batter covers the entire surface. Bubbles of varying sizes (sometimes called "eyes") should appear in the batter very close together. (If the bubbles are scattered, the batter needs to ferment for another day.)

Cover the pan with a lid and cook without flipping until the injera is cooked through, 2 to 3 minutes Remove with a spatula.

Cool completely in a single layer on a clean tablecloth or towel.

Storage Stack the cooled injera and store at room temperature for up to 2 days, or wrap individually in plastic wrap, stack in a zip-top plastic bag, and freeze for up to 3 weeks.

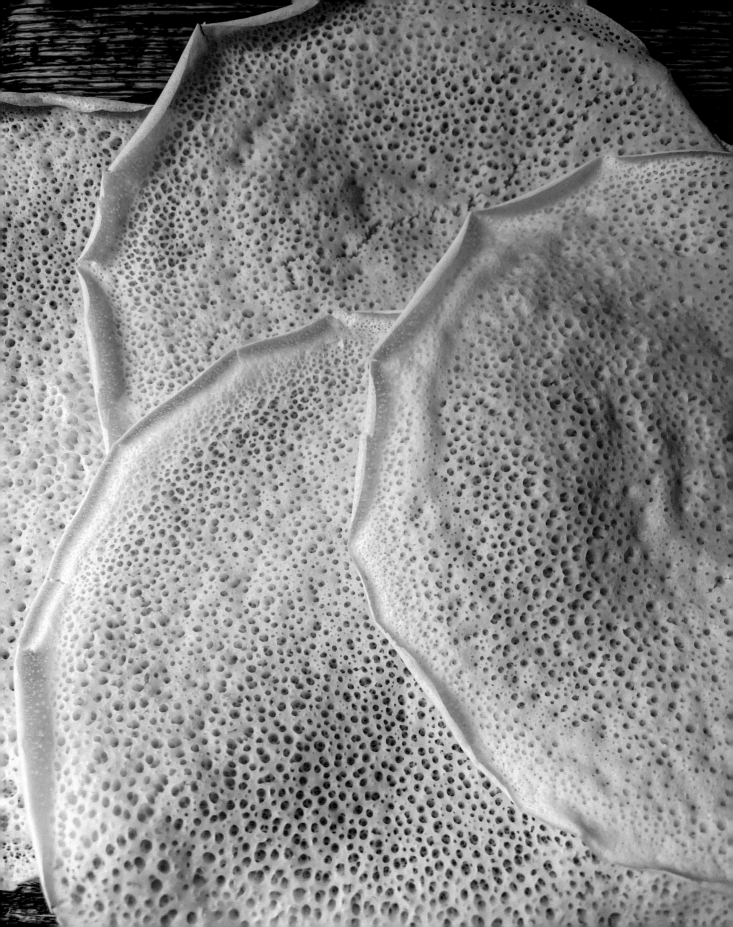

KATEGNA

Injera Treat

Makes 2 treats

Kategna is the Ethiopian Jewish cook's treat, the savory ending to a batch of injera. My mother used to pour the last of the batter onto the surface of the hot pan, dollop on some niter kibbeh and hot sauce, sprinkle on a dusting of berbere, and place it in my waiting hands, something to keep my stomach from growling until the full meal was served. I now love doing the same for my children.

¼ cup Niter Kibbeh (page 15), melted

1 tablespoon Berbere (page 5)

2 (10-inch) Injera (page 37)

2 teaspoons Awaze (page 32; optional)

IN A SMALL BOWL, mix the niter kibbeh and berbere.

Warm a 12-inch nonstick pan over high heat. Lay one injera in the pan and cook until the bottom is crisp and the edges are curling, about 1 minute.

Transfer to a serving plate. Use a spoon to spread half the niter kibbeh–berbere mix over the top of the injera. Drizzle with the awaze (if using).

Repeat with the other injera and remaining butter-berbere mix. Serve immediately.

NAY KEDAM DABO / MESWAIT

Genet's Pot-Baked Shabbat Bread

Makes 1 large loaf (serves 10 to 12)

My aunt Genet (Ilana) Mamay (page 219) remembers fondly how her family celebrated Shabbat in the village of Walkeit, in the southern part of Ethiopia. Her family made their dabo by placing the dough in a ceramic pot and burying it in hot coals and wood. Today, when they come to visit, Genet bakes this fragrant, spice-infused shabbat dabo in a similar way—but in a pot on the stove. This method creates a gorgeous, bronzed bread with a hint of smoke and heady undertones of fenugreek, coriander, and cardamom. It tastes exquisite. Don't worry if it doesn't turn out perfectly round or smooth. Its rustic quality is part of the charm. It's delicious in Dabo Fit-Fit / Crumbled Dabo with Spices (page 74), which Genet also makes every Sabbath.

- 2 pounds (907 grams) spelt flour
- 2 tablespoons granulated sugar or brown sugar
- 2¼ teaspoons (1 envelope) instant yeast
- 1 teaspoon fine sea salt
- ½ teaspoon ground fenugreek
- ½ teaspoon ground coriander
- ½ teaspoon ground cardamom
- 2½ cups (600 grams) warm water, plus more if necessary
- 1 tablespoon vegetable oil, plus more for drizzling

IN A LARGE BOWL, mix the flour, sugar, yeast, salt, fenugreek, coriander, and cardamom. Add the warm water, ½ cup at a time, working the water into the flour until a dough forms. Knead the oil into the dough until it is wet and elastic. If it seems too dry, add more water, a tablespoon at a time.

Cover with a damp towel and place in a warm place until doubled in size and light and bubbly on top, 1 to 2 hours.

Line a medium cast-iron pot or Dutch oven with two layers of parchment paper and drizzle the paper with oil. Transfer the dough to the pot and use wet hands to spread it into an even layer and smooth out the surface. Cover with the lid and let rise for about 15 minutes.

With the pot still covered, set it over low heat and cook for 25 minutes. Use the top layer of parchment paper to lift the bread out of the pot. Place on a plate. Drizzle the uncooked top with oil, then return the bread oiled-side down to the pot on top of the second layer of parchment paper, and drizzle the other (cooked) side with oil.

Cook until the bread is golden brown and puffed and the center reaches about 190°F on an instant-read thermometer, about 25 minutes.

DABO / HIBSIT

Spiced Whole Wheat Bread

Makes 1 large loaf (serves 10 to 12)

Avejo Aklum (page 101), my cousin and the sister of Ferede Aklum (page xxxi), grew up a little spoiled: Her parents had household staff, so she never needed to work in the kitchen at a young age. As an adult, she had a hard time mastering the cooking, to the point where her neighbors had to help her. She even had to buy injera from the store.

But Avejo became a good example of how hard work and attention can turn someone into an amazing cook. Today, she is known for having very blessed hands. Her stews are unique and her injera is instantly recognizable. And this dabo, which I adapted from her instructions, is an unusually well-seasoned, spiced version of our cherished Shabbat bread.

1½ tablespoons CH'ew Kemem (page 27)

1½ teaspoons sugar

1 teaspoon active dry yeast

½ teaspoon fine sea salt

2 cups (480 grams) warm water

3 cups (420 grams) bread flour

1 cup (140 grams) coarse whole wheat flour

IN A MEDIUM BOWL, combine the CH'ew kemem, sugar, yeast, and sea salt. Add the warm water and stir until well combined. Add the bread flour and whole wheat flour and knead until the dough is smooth and sticky, 6 to 8 minutes.

Shape the dough into a ball, cover the bowl with plastic wrap, place a towel on top, and let it sit in a warm place until doubled in size, about 1 hour.

Line a sheet pan or 9-inch baking pan with parchment paper. Punch down the dough, shape into a neat ball, and place on the prepared pan. Cover with plastic wrap, place a towel on top, and let sit in a warm place until the dough has puffed up, 1 hour to 1½ hours.

Preheat the oven to 400°F.

Uncover the pan and bake until lightly browned on top, 30 to 40 minutes. Cool for about 5 minutes, then remove from the pan to a rack and cool completely before serving.

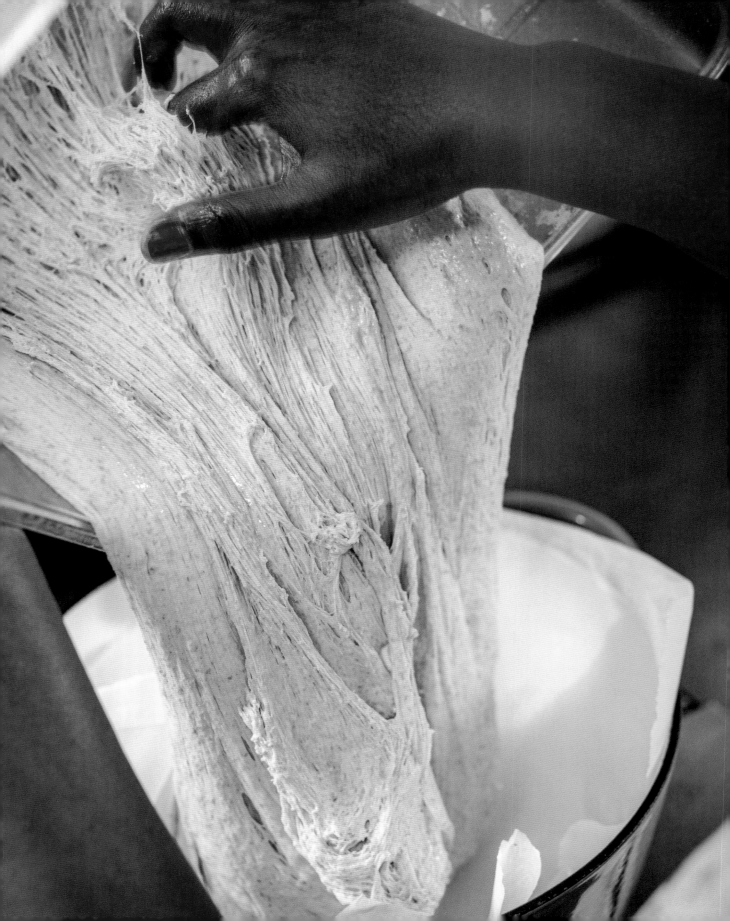

YA FASSIKAH KITA / NAY WURENAH KICHA

Ethiopian Matzah

Makes 3 to 4 large matzahs

Feel free to use just one type of teff flour in this special Ethiopian matzah that is suitable for Passover because it does not rise, leaven, or ferment. My grandmother made it every morning during Passover, mixing the batter right after she woke up and serving the matzah for breakfast. My family adhered so strictly to Jewish law that they ate it plain or with flaxseed: Less stringent eaters may enjoy it with Niter Kibbeh (page 15).

½ cup (115 grams) ivory teff flour

½ cup (115 grams) brown teff flour

1 teaspoon fine sea salt

2 cups (480 grams) lukewarm water

1 tablespoon vegetable oil (omit if using a nonstick pan)

IN A LARGE BOWL, use your hands to combine the teff flours, salt, and luke warm water, breaking up clumps of flour, until smooth.

Warm a 12-inch skillet over high heat. If the skillet does not have a nonstick coating, add the oil and swirl to coat the pan.

Pour 1 cup batter into the center of the pan and use the bottom of a ladle to spread it over the surface of the pan. Cook until dry on top, about 3 minutes. Push a wide spatula underneath the matzah, and carefully flip it over. Reduce the heat to medium-low and cook until the matzah is completely cooked through, about 3 minutes. Repeat with the remaining batter. Serve immediately.

KITA / *KICHA*

Flatbread for a Journey

Makes about 3 flatbreads

This is what you make when you need simple, delicious bread quickly. It requires no rising or fermenting, and can easily be made on the road. Even during the most harrowing moments in our journeys, my family always spent Friday afternoons looking for a source of water so we could prepare this flatbread and observe the Sabbath. This is designed to be eaten right away: It does not store as well as other breads.

IN A LARGE BOWL, use your hands to mix the flour, salt, and 1½ cups (355 grams) water together until the mixture becomes a thick batter.

Warm a large nonstick skillet over medium heat. Add ½ teaspoon niter kibbeh and spread it over the surface of the pan to coat. Pour in about ½ cup batter and spread it over the surface of the skillet, using wet hands to push it to the edges if necessary. Cover and steam until the top starts to look dry, the edges are defined, and bottom is turning golden, 2 to 4 minutes. Flip over and cook until the bottom is golden, about another 2 minutes. Repeat with the remaining batter and niter kibbeh.

Serve plain, or drizzle with niter kibbeh and top with spices. Serve immediately.

- 2 cups (260 grams) all-purpose flour
- ¼ teaspoon fine sea salt
- 1½ teaspoons Niter Kibbeh (page 15), unsalted butter, or vegetable oil

OPTIONAL TOPPINGS

Niter kibbeh

Mitmita (page 12)

Berbere (page 5)

PORTRAIT

ASTER SOLOMON
Surviving the Famine

When many people think of Ethiopia, they immediately think of the famine of the mid-1980s. They remember images of starving children and adults, a rising death toll, a drought that made it all but impossible to survive. By that point, the vast majority of my family (including me) had already moved to Israel.

Except for Aster Solomon, my grandmother's niece. Aster had not joined any of the groups making their way out of Ethiopia because she had just gotten married to a local blacksmith. She was pregnant with her first child when the family's crops began to dry up. Food disappeared from the market. Red Cross workers encouraged Aster and her husband to travel toward Sudan.

But the expecting couple was understandably hesitant to travel with a child on the way. They figured they would stay for the birth, and hope that in the meantime there would be a dramatic change in the weather. After all, Aster said, she grew up putting little seeds into the ground, popping yellow chickpeas into her mouth, being part of a community that was constantly planting and gathering. She could not imagine that that might be gone forever.

But the people had largely left, and Aster and her husband watched in horror as the food became scarcer and scarcer. They scrounged for water and planted seeds in vain. They survived mostly on porridge made from stored millet. They longed for their community, now so far away, wondering if Aster and her family were OK. When her daughter was born, miraculously healthy, they named her Hesve, which means "my people." They watched their friends suffer. One neighbor, Aster recalls, had such limited grain that he often had to choose between feeding his mother and feeding his young child.

These desperate times lasted for three long years. Once the famine ended in 1985, Aster and her husband rejoiced at the sight of crops inching through the newly moist earth. While they could now eat freely, they finally decided to leave their home and land because the rebel group in Northern Ethiopia permitted them to journey freely toward Sudan without having to do so under cover of darkness. In Sudan, former neighbors helped them adjust, and they were eventually added to the Mossad's list of refugees.

And so they did embark on a journey in the middle of the night. Israeli commandos landed a helicopter outside where they were staying, stormed in, picked them up, and flew them straight to Tel Aviv. Aster remembers that commandos offered them Israeli salad and pickles, but they were so excited that they didn't have an appetite. When they landed at Ben Gurion airport in May 1987, Aster saw her relatives for the first time in years, and knew that she was finally in good hands. Her family was safe. What's more, she was pregnant again. She gave birth to her second child later that year.

From there, Aster's life got much easier. Because the Beta Israel community was already so established, she had plenty of people to show her how to make berbere and injera and help her care for her family. She even figured out the Israeli public

ASTER'S DISH

transportation system all on her own and took a bus for a surprise reunion with my grandmother, her beloved aunt. She remembers my grandmother's words: "How did you get here? How did you manage to make it? I'm so glad to see you."

My grandmother's words sum up Aster's story beautifully. How did she manage to make it through so many obstacles? How did she survive under the most dramatic of circumstances? How did she become what she is today, a grandmother living happily in southern Israel? For me, Aster's story represents the resilience of the Beta Israel community, who all pushed through the darkest of days and lived to see a new beginning.

LOUDO

Niger Seed Bread

Makes 1 large flatbread (serves 4 to 6)

The moment I bite into this bread, covered with dark, earthy niger seeds, I immediately return to my childhood in Ethiopia and my journey to Sudan. Because niger seeds are so nutritious and portable, we relied heavily on them during our travels, and we often nibbled on them for Passover. This bread came up in a recent conversation with my grandmother's niece Aster Solomon (page 59) and my aunt Terfinish Ferede, who reported that it was a favorite of my grandmother's, too. Re-creating it felt like an important connection to my past, the resurrection of an ancient recipe that is so simple and so distinctively delicious.

½ cup niger seeds, picked over for any hulls or debris

½ teaspoon Berbere (page 5)

¾ teaspoon fine sea salt

1 cup (140 grams) sorghum flour, stone-ground if possible

1 cup (130 grams) all-purpose flour

½ teaspoon baking powder

¼ teaspoon CH'ew Kemem (page 27)

Vegetable oil, for greasing the pan

WARM A MEDIUM SKILLET over low heat. Add the niger seeds and toast, stirring constantly, until the seeds are fragrant and take on a white-golden tinge, about 5 minutes. The seeds will make a light popping sound while toasting. Transfer the seeds to a plate and cool completely.

Transfer the seeds to a spice grinder and grind into a powder. Sift the seed powder through a fine-mesh strainer into a small bowl. Discard any hulls in the strainer. Combine the seeds, berbere, ¼ teaspoon of the salt, and ¼ cup (60 grams) water until a paste forms. Set aside.

In a medium bowl, combine the sorghum flour, all-purpose flour, baking powder, remaining ½ teaspoon salt, and the CH'ew kemem. Add 1¼ cups (300 grams) cold water and knead until a dough forms.

Lightly oil an 8- or 9-inch nonstick skillet and warm over low heat. Place a small bowl of water near the stove for wetting your hands. Transfer all the dough to the pan and use your wet hands to press it into an even layer that covers the entire surface of the pan.

Cook the bread until firm around the edges, about 5 minutes. Use your wet hands to spread the seed paste all over the flatbread. Cover the pan and cook until the center of the bread is set and the edges have puffed a little, another 5 minutes. Remove with a spatula and cool on a serving plate.

Note To make gluten-free loudo, swap out the cup of all-purpose flour for an additional cup of sorghum flour.

HANZA

Layered Yellow Corn Bread

Makes 4 or 5 layered breads

This hanza is influenced by two people: my mother, who was well known for making this distinctive Tigrayan corn-based flatbread, and her close friend Mehrata (Malka) Lemlem Avraham (page 174), who recently taught me how to make this dish. It uses two types of corn: finely milled corn flour and more coarsely ground cornmeal, for texture.

DAY 1

In a large container with a lid, mix the corn flour and warm water. Cover and let sit at room temperature for 24 hours.

DAY 2

There will not be any visible changes to the batter.

In a small pot, boil 1 cup water over medium-high heat. Divide the batter into four parts by making a cross with your finger in the batter. Scoop out one-quarter of the batter and whisk it into the pot of boiling water. Reduce the heat to medium-low and stir frequently as the mixture thickens, first to a doughy texture, then to a smooth, silky dough that pulls away from the sides of the pot, 8 to 10 minutes. Cool completely.

To the remaining three-quarters of the batter, stir in the cornmeal, all-purpose flour, sugar, oil, salt, fenugreek, and 1 cup water. Knead well. Add the cooled dough and another 1 cup water and mix until smooth: The texture will be like that of thick pancake batter. Cover and keep in a dark cool place for 24 hours.

DAY 3

By day 3, the mixture should have bubbles of varying sizes and a yogurty, lactic acid smell. The surface of the batter will be lumpy, shiny, and bubbly. (If this is not the case, the batter needs more time to ferment.)

TO COOK

Whisk the batter, then stream in ½ cup (120 grams) water while whisking constantly. Whisk in the baking powder. The batter should be loose like the texture of drinkable yogurt. Test the

4 cups (400 grams) corn flour

3 cups (720 grams) warm water

1 cup (128 grams) coarsely ground cornmeal

2 cups (260 grams) all-purpose flour

1 tablespoon sugar

1 tablespoon vegetable oil

1 teaspoon fine sea salt

½ teaspoon ground fenugreek

½ teaspoon baking powder

FOR COOKING AND SERVING

About 10 tablespoons Niter Kibbeh (page 15)

¼ cup Mitmita (page 12) or mitmita paste (see Note)

Awaze (page 32), for serving

Hanza continues

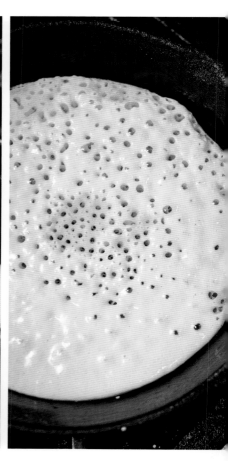

consistency: Lift the whisk out of the batter and let the excess drip back into the bowl. It should blend in and not sit on top of the surface. If it sits on top of the batter, whisk in water, 1 tablespoon at a time.

In an 8- or 9-inch scratch-free nonstick skillet, ladle 1 cup batter and rotate your wrist in a circular motion until the batter covers the entire surface of the pan. You will see bubbles or "eyes" appear on the surface, which should be visible across the batter. Cover with a lid and cook undisturbed (without flipping) for 3 minutes. Move the cooked hanza to a plate.

Spread 2 tablespoons of niter kibbeh over the warm hanza, followed by ½ teaspoon of mitmita (or spread 1 teaspoon of the paste, if you like). Begin cooking another hanza and about halfway through the cooking time, flip the seasoned, completed hanza on top ("eyes" facing downward) of the cooking hanza so the spices and niter kibbeh meld. Continue cooking for another 5 minutes and flip again. Remove from the pan and set aside on a serving plate and cut into slices. Repeat with the remaining batter.

Note To make a spreadable paste of the mitma, mix ¼ cup mitmita with 2 tablespoons Tej (page 180), white wine, or water. Serve immediately. Wrap any left over and store for up to 1 day.

VARIATION

Anebabero (typical among the Amhara people): Cook 2 hanzas without the addition of the niter kibbeh or mitmita. As the second hanza finishes cooking, spread ¼ cup of batter between two individual hanzas. Cook for 10 minutes on each side until firm. Remove from the pan and spread generously with 3 to 4 tablespoons of niter kibbeh on both sides and sprinkle (or spread) mitmita on top. In this tradition, the eyes are left facing outward to soak in all the niter kibbeh and the berbere.

ASEFASH'S LACHUCH

Soft Yemenite Flatbread

Makes 6 flatbreads

This soft, spongy Yemenite flatbread played a big role in the journey of Asefash Mesele (page 148), one of the first Beta Israel to journey from Ethiopia to Israel. Her husband had gone to study in Israel in the 1950s, before returning to Ethiopia and marrying Asefash. The two lived for a time in Eritrea before taking a boat to Israel in 1968. When they arrived, they were one of only a few families from Ethiopia. Not only was it nearly impossible to find ingredients to make Ethiopian food, it was also difficult to store them, as refrigeration was uncommon.

However, Asefash and her husband found a community among the Yemenites who had already immigrated to Israel. These more established immigrants helped Asefash take care of her children, and they taught her how to make this flatbread, which could be made in a single day and was the closest thing to injera that she could initially eat in Israel.

IN A MEDIUM BOWL, whisk the semolina and 1 cup of the warm water together until combined. Let the batter sit until the flour has softened and the mixture is the consistency of porridge, about 30 minutes.

In a large bowl, mix the yeast, sugar, and remaining 1¼ cups warm water. Let stand until bubbly, about 5 minutes. Stir in the semolina mixture, all-purpose flour, salt, and fenugreek. Whisk well for about 1 minute, cover, and let sit in a warm place in your kitchen until bubbly, about 30 minutes.

Whisk in the baking powder for 30 seconds. Cover with plastic wrap, place a towel on top, and let stand until bubbles cover the surface of the batter, about 30 minutes.

Warm a 7-inch nonstick skillet over medium heat. Pour a small amount of oil into the pan and wipe the excess out with a paper towel. Whisk the batter, then ladle ½ cup into the pan. Swirl the pan so the batter covers the entire bottom of the pan. Large compact bubbles should appear across the surface of the batter. (If bubbles don't appear, the mixture needs more resting time: Cover

1 cup (160 grams) semolina flour

2¼ cups (540 grams) warm water

1 teaspoon active dry yeast

1 teaspoon sugar

1 cup (130 grams) all-purpose flour

2 teaspoons fine sea salt

1½ teaspoons ground fenugreek

1 teaspoon baking powder

Vegetable oil, for pan-frying

Asefash's Lachuch continues

---

and return to the warm place for another 30 minutes or until bubbly and active.)

After 2 minutes, cover the pan with a lid and cook until the flatbread is springy and firm to the touch. Transfer to a plate.

Continue with the next lachuch, oiling and wiping the pan after each one.

Storage Place in a single layer and cool completely before wrapping in plastic wrap and stacking in a resealable plastic bag. Store in the refrigerator for up to 4 days.

KOLO

Crunchy Ethiopian Snack Mix

Makes about 1½ cups

⅓ cup dried desi (small) chickpeas (or regular dried chickpeas; see Note)

1 cup wheat berries

¼ cup sunflower seeds

¼ teaspoon fine sea salt

Optional additions: ¼ cup roasted peanuts and/or golden raisins

About 1 teaspoon Mitmita (page 12) or Berbere (page 5), optional

When we had no bread during our journey to Sudan, we munched on this while drinking coffee and pictured better days ahead in Israel. This crunchy combination of legumes, grains, and seeds is one of the most cherished types of what we call *senki* in Tigrinya—"journey food." Senki are portable and don't spoil easily. Roasting the chickpeas, wheat berries, and sunflower seeds individually brings out their oils and fills your kitchen with the deep fragrance you'd miss if they were left raw. While this mix will last for months in an airtight container, my family often eats it right away. Desi chickpeas are smaller, darker chickpeas and are available online or at Ethiopian or Indian grocery stores.

IN A SMALL BOWL, cover the chickpeas with water by about 1 inch and soak at room temperature while you prepare the rest of the ingredients.

Heat a cast-iron skillet over medium heat. Add the wheat berries in a single layer and roast undisturbed until you hear the first pop, about 90 seconds. Stir constantly until the wheat berries are a deep golden brown, about 3 minutes. Spread out on a tray in an even layer to cool.

Return the skillet to medium heat and add the sunflower seeds. Stir constantly (the seeds will pop) until the seeds are dark, about 3 minutes. Transfer to the tray with the wheat berries and spread in an even layer.

Return the skillet to medium heat. Drain the chickpeas and add to the pan. Sprinkle with the sea salt and stir constantly until darkened and fragrant, about 3 minutes. Transfer to the tray with the wheat berries and sunflower seeds. If desired, add the peanuts and/or raisins in an even layer. Sprinkle with the mitmita or berbere (if using). Cool completely.

Storage Store in an airtight container at room temperature for up to 3 months.

Note If you use larger dried chickpeas, you may need to adjust the soaking and cooking time.

CHAPTER 3

SUNRISE SUSTENANCE

Ethiopian breakfast is colorful, highly nutritious, and a source of deep comfort, whether you're waking up to the sound of a crackling fire and roasting coffee, or mixing up a bowl of porridge on a long journey, or settling into a country far from Ethiopia. In this chapter, I share with you the anchors of an Ethiopian morning.

DABO FIT-FIT
Crumbled Dabo with Spices
Serves 4

4½ cups Nay Kedam Dabo (page 51), broken into bite-sized pieces (about one-third of the recipe), or another bread, ideally a day old

1 cup sour cream or plain yogurt

1 cup Nay Habesha Selata (page 88)

1 tablespoon Niter Kibbeh (page 15)

1 teaspoon Berbere (page 5)

½ teaspoon fine sea salt, plus more to taste

½ teaspoon black pepper, plus more to taste

Welcome to the Ethiopian tradition of fit-fits, a cherished custom that mixes leftover bread with salad and spices for a satisfying breakfast (or an on-the-go snack for a journey or picnic) that is even more than the sum of its parts.

Dabo fit-fit is what the Beta Israel community eats for breakfast on Saturday morning after synagogue. Our ancient tradition decrees that we do not eat hot food on the Shabbat: We do not believe in starting fires on Friday and continuing them on Saturday. Instead, we make our dabo on Thursday, and on Saturday mix together a simple salad to toss with bread for a moist, saucy breakfast. Some of my most cherished childhood memories are of going to sleep on Friday in great anticipation of breakfast, then awakening on Saturday morning to a spread of salads and bread pieces. I was permitted to build my own fit-fit, with all the spices and colors that I desired. In that spirit, I've given you starting points for your own fit-fit here. Feel free to add more or less of what sounds good to you.

IN A LARGE BOWL, mix the dabo pieces with the sour cream, Ethiopian salad, niter kibbeh, berbere, salt, and pepper. Mix gently. Taste and adjust the seasoning, if necessary.

INJERA FIR-FIR
Ripped Injera with Silsi
Serves 4

½ cup Kulet (page 5)

2 (10-inch) Injera (page 37), torn into bite-sized pieces

2 teaspoons Niter Kibbeh (page 15)

Fine sea salt and black pepper

2 teaspoons diced tomato

2 teaspoons diced jalapeño

2 tablespoons Ayib (page 18), plain yogurt, or sour cream

Here's a quick, simple preparation of fir-fir for when you have leftover injera.

IN A LARGE SKILLET, warm the kulet over medium heat until sizzling. Add the injera and mix until evenly coated and warmed through. Mix in the niter kibbeh and salt and pepper to taste. Add the tomato and jalapeño and sauté until softened, about 2 minutes. Garnish with the ayib, yogurt, or sour cream.

SUFF FIT-FIT

Injera Rolls with Sunflower Seed Dressing

Serves 4

Here's a dressed-up version of injera fir-fir, in which the bread is rolled up and soaked with a nutty liquid made from sunflower seeds.

IN A SHALLOW BOWL, combine the suff base, onion, garlic, jalapeño, olive oil, berbere, lemon juice, and salt and mix gently. Place the injera rolls in the liquid, cut-side up, and arrange the tomato slices on top. Garnish with the cilantro and a squeeze of lemon or lime juice and more jalapeño, if desired. Soak for at least 5 minutes before serving: the injera will gradually absorb all the liquid.

3 cups Suff Base (page 28)

1 red onion, finely chopped

2 garlic cloves, minced

1 jalapeño, sliced, plus more (optional) for garnish

1 tablespoon olive oil

1 teaspoon Berbere (page 5)

1 teaspoon fresh lemon juice, plus more (optional) for serving

½ teaspoon fine salt

1 (10-inch) Injera (page 37), rolled up, then cut crosswise into ½-inch rolls

1 tomato, halved and sliced into half-moons

½ cup fresh cilantro leaves and tender stems, chopped

KITA FIR-FIR / *KICHA FIR-FIR*

Crumbled Flatbread with Sour Cream

Serves 4

In this version, leftover flatbread gets spiced up with leftover stew base for a satisfying breakfast.

IN A LARGE SKILLET, warm the kulet over medium heat until sizzling. Mix with the kita until evenly coated and warmed through. Mix in the niter kibbeh and salt and pepper to taste. Add the tomato and jalapeño and sauté until softened, about 2 minutes. Garnish with the sour cream.

½ cup Kulet (page 6)

2 Kita (page 58), torn into bite-sized pieces

2 teaspoons Niter Kibbeh (page 15)

Fine sea salt and black pepper

2 teaspoons diced tomato

2 teaspoons diced jalapeño

2 tablespoons sour cream

KINCHE

Savory Steel-Cut Oat Porridge

Serves 4

For the Beta Israel community, breakfast is not sweet, and that includes porridge. This savory oatmeal is our breakfast ideal. It is often made with bulgur wheat, but this version substitutes steel-cut oats, which have a similar texture. If you'd like a little sweetness, try sprinkling on a few raisins and pistachios or cashews.

IN A MEDIUM POT, combine 3 cups water, the oil, and salt and bring to a boil over medium heat. Add the oats, cover, reduce the heat to low, and simmer, stirring occasionally, until the oats are tender and have absorbed the water, about 45 minutes.

Transfer to a serving bowl. Drizzle the niter kibbeh on top and garnish with the jalapeño and berbere. Serve warm.

- 1 tablespoon vegetable oil
- ¼ teaspoon fine sea salt
- 2 cups steel-cut oats, rinsed until the water runs nearly clear
- ¼ cup Niter Kibbeh (page 15), melted
- ½ jalapeño, finely chopped
- ½ teaspoon Berbere (page 5)

ALEMASH TESSMA
The Resilience of the Female Spirit

The story of Alemash Tessma demonstrates the power of women banding together to help each other through life's challenges.

Alemash, my grandmother's niece, led a charmed life on a beautiful, prosperous family farm in Tigray until she was four. But that came to an abrupt end when the farm was destroyed in a jealous act of rage by other villagers and Alemash's mother was killed in the attack.

As a result, Alemash was raised by her grandmother, a midwife. Her grandmother believed that her work was a mitzvah, a blessing, something that Alemash could carry on in her own life to spread joy throughout the world. And so, from a very young age, each time a woman went into labor in their village, Alemash followed her grandmother to help.

The true beauty of giving birth in Ethiopia was that a new mother never needed to worry about food, taking care of her baby, or taking care of the rest of her family while she recovered from childbirth. The whole village cared for them.

The Beta Israel provided a network of support that helped new mothers heal, connect with their baby, and come back to their families energized. This community was so strong that Alemash says she often witnessed women compete as to who would be the first to feed the new mother.

Alemash told me about the rituals that began as soon as a woman went into labor. Once the baby was delivered and the umbilical cord was cut, something hot to eat and drink was given to the mother. Gaat, a porridge made of teff and clarified butter, and/or telva, a flaxseed drink, was provided to give her strength and sustenance. Soon after her waist was wrapped, she was rubbed with oils, and allowed to rest. Finally, the women attending to the new mother sang the call that the rest of the village had been waiting for, the announcement of the baby's birth. "EL EL EL . . . ," they would sing, chanting twelve times if the baby was a boy, nine times for a girl.

Then would begin the sacred weeks following childbirth. The new mother stayed in a special house, known as the Harrase Gojo ("The House of the New Mother"), and focused on resting and bonding with her baby. Meanwhile, the other women in the community guided her on how to breastfeed her child, kept her company to keep her from being depressed, and, if the baby was a boy, arranged for his circumcision when he was eight days old. They also did her family's cooking and clothes washing, minded her older children, and performed other tasks so that she could focus on resting and bonding with her baby.

If the baby was a boy, the woman stayed in the Gojo for forty days; after the birth of a girl, eighty days. This time culminated with a village-wide feast that welcomed the newborn and the mother back home.

Alemash's description of these Beta Israel rituals made me envious: I wished that I had had that kind of network when I had my children in New York. I was lucky enough to have had my mother come from Israel to take care of me and make me food.

But I know many people here who gave birth with little support and guidance, who would have benefited greatly from these rituals.

Alemash faced many obstacles in her journey to have her own family. She and her husband were already the parents of two, with a third on the way, when they began preparing to travel to Israel in the 1970s. But then her husband suddenly got sick and passed away, leaving her a widow with three young children, about to leave the only home she had ever known.

In 1978, she and her children joined a 240-person group that traveled from Ethiopia to Sudan. Alemash and her children stayed in Sudan for a few years and, in 1981, embarked on a lengthy journey to Israel. The Israeli military escorted them on a boat through the Red Sea, then they took buses through Egypt, and finally they flew to Tel Aviv, en route to their final destination of Ashkelon.

When they arrived, they initially had nowhere to stay, thanks to a mix-up at the immigration center. Alemash spent the first few confusing days with distant family members before getting a place of her own.

Even more unsettling, she also found that Israeli laws prohibited her from helping deliver babies—the only career she had ever known.

However, again Alemash endured. Slowly she integrated into Israeli society. She remarried and had more children. She started her own business selling beauty products, while informally providing support to new mothers. Eventually, she managed to buy her own house. I am so proud and inspired by her ability to build a life for herself and help others in their most trying times.

GENFO / GAAT

Hearty Teff Porridge

Serves 4

This hearty porridge is not only a quick breakfast any time you'd like, it also represents new beginnings. It is the traditional sustenance served to new brides and pregnant women when they go into labor and then give birth. I love stirring the thick mixture—it's good for your biceps! The cooked porridge is typically molded into a bowl, then flipped over for a smooth top. This takes a bit of practice, so I recommend just serving it in a bowl.

1 teaspoon fine sea salt

1½ cups teff flour

1 tablespoon plus ¼ teaspoon Niter Kibbeh (page 15)

½ teaspoon Berbere (page 5)

IN A NONSTICK MEDIUM POT, combine 3 cups water and the salt and bring to a boil over medium-high heat. Using a heatproof measuring cup, remove about 1 cup of boiling water and transfer to a bowl. Set aside.

Stir the teff flour into the pot, reduce the heat to medium, and use a wooden spoon or heatproof silicone spatula to vigorously mix into a thick, wet paste: Stirring quickly will prevent lumps from forming. Add ½ cup of the reserved water and mix in for about a minute, until well incorporated and smooth. Cover and let cook for about 2 minutes. Mix in another ¼ cup water and repeat, mixing for a minute or two. Cover and let cook for about 2 minutes. Add the remaining ¼ cup water and vigorously stir for about 1 minute. Cover and cook until the porridge looks like a thick, wet dough and easily forms into a ball, about 3 minutes.

In the bottom of a medium serving bowl, place ¼ teaspoon of the niter kibbeh. Scoop the porridge on top and use a spoon to smooth the top. Spoon a hole in the middle and place the remaining 1 tablespoon niter kibbeh in the middle. Sprinkle the berbere on top.

ATMIT / SIBKO

Banana Flour Porridge

Serves 2

This thin, nutritious porridge is made with the powdered root of the enset plant, also known as bula, or false banana, an enormous crop in Ethiopia. In addition to being abundant and nutritious, atmit is also a delicious way to stay warm in wintertime, or to nourish yourself when you are feeling under the weather. Some people eat this with clarified butter. I like sipping it from a mug, with honey and a little bit of cinnamon. Bula can be mail-ordered or found at Ethiopian stores.

¼ cup oat flour

2 teaspoons bula (banana flour)

2 tablespoons honey (optional), or to taste

Pinch of ground cinnamon (optional)

IN A SMALL BOWL, whisk together the oat flour and 1 cup water until well combined, about 1 minute.

In a small pot, bring 1½ cups water to a boil over high heat. Pour the oat/water mixture through a fine-mesh strainer into the pot. Stir well, bring to a boil, reduce the heat to medium-low, and simmer until the mixture thickens slightly, about 5 minutes.

In a small bowl, whisk the bula with ½ cup water. Slowly stream the mixture into the pot, whisking constantly. Increase the heat to medium and cook until the porridge is vigorously bubbling and a much thicker, gravy-like consistency, about 5 minutes. Serve hot, topped with honey or cinnamon to taste, if desired.

FUL ### Stewed Fava Beans

Here are two ways to use the nutritious, protein-packed fava beans that I ate for breakfast as a child. The version that starts with dried beans takes time and patience, but the flavor cannot be beat. Using canned beans will cut more than an hour off the process and still result in a satisfying meal.

DRIED BEAN FUL *Serves 6 to 8*

SOAK THE DRIED BEANS in water to cover for at least 30 minutes and preferably overnight. Drain the beans.

In a large pot, combine the beans and water to cover by 1 inch. Cover the pot, bring to a boil over medium heat, and cook until you can bite through the beans, about 45 minutes.

Stir in the kulet, cumin, salt, and pepper. Cover the pot, reduce the heat to medium-low, and simmer, stirring occasionally, until the beans are very soft, about 1 hour 15 minutes, adding up to ½ cup more water if necessary to prevent sticking.

Transfer to a food processor and blend until smooth. Taste and add more salt, if necessary.

Transfer to a shallow serving bowl and garnish with the eggs, red onion, jalapeño, tomato, ayib, and a drizzle of niter kibbeh or olive oil. Serve with the kita.

1 pound dried large fava beans

¼ cup Kulet (page 6)

1 teaspoon ground cumin

½ teaspoon fine sea salt, plus more to taste

½ teaspoon black pepper

GARNISHES

2 hard-boiled eggs, quartered

2 heaping tablespoons diced red onion

2 heaping tablespoons chopped jalapeño pepper

2 heaping tablespoons chopped tomato

2 tablespoons Ayib (page 18) or crumbled feta cheese

Niter Kibbeh (page 15), melted, or olive oil, for drizzling

Kita (page 58), for dipping

Ful continues

CANNED BEAN FUL

Serves 6 to 8

IN A LARGE SKILLET, combine the beans and their liquid, kulet, cumin, salt, pepper, and niter kibbeh. Bring to a simmer over medium heat, stirring frequently and coarsely mashing the beans with a wooden spoon, and cook until thickened, 8 to 10 minutes.

Transfer to a shallow serving bowl and garnish with the eggs, onion, jalapeño, tomato, ayib, and a drizzle of niter kibbeh or olive oil. Serve with the kita.

2 (16-ounce) cans fava beans, undrained

¼ cup Kulet (page 6)

1 teaspoon ground cumin

½ teaspoon fine sea salt

½ teaspoon black pepper

1 tablespoon Niter Kibbeh (page 15), melted

GARNISHES

2 hard-boiled eggs, quartered

2 heaping tablespoons diced red onion

2 heaping tablespoons chopped jalapeño

2 heaping tablespoons chopped tomato

2 tablespoons Ayib (page 18) or crumbled feta cheese

Niter Kibbeh (page 15), melted, or olive oil, for drizzling

Kita (page 58), for dipping

ENQULAL TIBS / *ENQUAQUHO TIBSI*

Scrambled Eggs with Tomato, Red Onion, and Jalapeño

Serves 2 to 4

Instead of making an omelet, try this hearty vegetable-filled scrambled eggs with Ethiopian flavors. It's very nutritious and can keep you filled up well into the day, particularly when served with injera.

IN A LARGE NONSTICK SKILLET, warm the oil over medium heat. Add the jalapeño, onion, and tomato and sauté until just softened, about 2 minutes.

In a medium bowl, beat the eggs, berbere, turmeric, salt, and black pepper. Add to the skillet and scramble until the eggs are cooked through.

If desired, drizzle with the niter kibbeh and serve over injera.

1 tablespoon olive oil

¼ cup minced jalapeño

¼ cup minced red onion

¼ cup diced tomato

4 large eggs

¼ teaspoon Berbere (page 5)
   Pinch of ground turmeric

⅛ teaspoon fine sea salt

⅛ teaspoon black pepper

¼ teaspoon Niter Kibbeh (page 15) or butter (optional), for drizzling

   Injera (page 37; optional), for serving

CHAPTER 4

VEGETABLES

In Ethiopia, my grandmother's niece Aster Solomon (page 59) recalls there being a season for every seed. Each season, the whole community, including the smallest children, came, planted, and gathered. Aster remembers that much of her childhood was spent putting little seeds into the ground. Her favorite crop? Tiny yellow chickpeas, which she popped into her mouth for a snack.

These recipes pay tribute to the colorful bounty that my family remembers from Tigray. They are the types of foods that we grew up eating and are proud to put on our tables today.

NAY HABESHA SELATA

Colorful Ethiopian Chopped Salad

Makes about 3 cups (serves 6, or more as a garnish)

This colorful salad, incorporating so many of the vegetables I grew up eating, is a crucial part of Dabo Fit-Fit (page 74) during Saturday Shabbat breakfast, but it's also lovely as a garnish or salad on its own.

IN A LARGE BOWL, gently combine the tomatoes, onion, cucumber, scallions, jalapeño, garlic, cilantro, and parsley. Add the olive oil, lemon juice, salt, and pepper and mix together. Serve at room temperature.

2 tomatoes, finely chopped

1 red onion, minced

½ cucumber or 2 Persian (mini) cucumbers, finely diced

2 scallions, minced

1 jalapeño, minced

4 garlic cloves, minced

1 tablespoon finely chopped fresh cilantro, leaves and tender stems

1 tablespoon finely chopped fresh parsley

1 tablespoon olive oil

Juice of ½ lemon, plus more to taste

¼ teaspoon fine sea salt, plus more to taste

¼ teaspoon black pepper, plus more to taste

TEMATIM SALATA / *KOMEDERO AVOCADO SELATA*

Tomato and Avocado Salad with Lemon and Cilantro

Serves 4 to 8

Light and refreshing, this is a salad to offer respite from the heat, often served as part of a large meal as an accent or garnish. However, it can easily be turned into an entrée for those days when it is too hot to turn on the stove: Tear leftover injera (or another bread) on top of the salad, let it soak up the tomato juice, lemon, and vinegar, and you have a filling vegan salad. Avocado adds a touch of luxurious richness.

———

IN A LARGE BOWL, combine the tomatoes, avocado, onion, and jalapeño. Gently mix in the lemon juice, salt, and pepper. Drizzle with olive oil and vinegar, sprinkle with cilantro, and mix gently. Serve at room temperature.

3 tomatoes, preferably vine-ripened, diced

1 avocado, diced

½ red onion, diced

1 jalapeño, minced

Juice of ½ lemon

¾ teaspoon fine sea salt

¼ teaspoon black pepper

2 tablespoons olive oil

1 tablespoon distilled white vinegar

4 sprigs fresh cilantro, leaves and thin stems, chopped

KARYA SINIG / *GUH*

Stuffed Jalapeño Peppers

Makes 5 to 10 stuffed peppers

Ethiopians like to eat spicy food so much that they will often just grab a serrano or jalapeño pepper and munch on it with dinner. This is an elevated version of that, which adds a pretty touch and gracious hospitality to the table. You can take a few minutes to assemble it while other food simmers, and leave it out at room temperature all day.

PLACE A JALAPEÑO on a cutting board. Split open in half lengthwise (taking care not to cut through the other side) and use a small spoon to scrape out the seeds and ribs (and discard). Repeat with the remaining peppers.

In a small bowl, mix the minced pepper, tomatoes, and onion. Mix in the lime or lemon juice, oil, salt, and black pepper. Spoon the filling into the split peppers.

If desired, crumble about 1 teaspoon cheese on top of each pepper.

5 large to 10 small jalapeño or serrano peppers, left whole, plus 1 jalapeño or serrano, minced

2 tomatoes, finely diced

1 red onion, finely diced

Juice of ½ lime or lemon

1 teaspoon olive oil

½ teaspoon fine sea salt

½ teaspoon black pepper

Optional garnish: 2 to 3 tablespoons crumbled Ayib (page 18) or feta cheese

MATBUCHA   Savory Tomato Salad

Serves 8 to 10

Matbucha, a chunky tomato-pepper salad, has roots in Israeli and Sephardic and North African cuisines. I adapted this recipe from a recipe from my cousin Vered Germay (page 8), who, in typical Israeli home cooking tradition, boosts the flavor with bouillon: Feel free to do so if you like.

IF USING FRESH TOMATOES, bring a large pot of water to a boil. Add the tomatoes and blanch until the skins begin peeling back from the flesh, about 2 minutes. Drain and shock the tomatoes under cold running water to stop the cooking. Peel the tomatoes, cut in half, and remove the stems. Cut into strips and add to a medium bowl.

If using canned tomatoes, cut into strips and add to a medium bowl along with the juices.

Over an open gas flame, char the bell pepper and jalapeños until blackened on all sides. Peel each under running water. Remove the stems and seeds, chop the peppers, and add both to the bowl of tomatoes.

In a dry medium pot, combine the onion and garlic and sauté over medium heat until the onions are slightly softened, about 5 minutes. Mix in the oil and sauté to combine for 5 minutes.

Stir in the tomato/pepper mixture, reduce the heat to low, bring to a simmer, and cook, stirring frequently, until the water has evaporated and the oil has risen to the top, about 1 hour.

Stir in the paprika, bouillon powder (if using), sugar, salt, black pepper, and turmeric. Simmer, stirring frequently to integrate the flavors, about 5 minutes.

At this point, if you prefer a smoother texture for the matbucha, use a potato masher or fork to process until smooth. Simmer until thickened, 10 to 15 minutes. Garnish with the cilantro and parsley.

- 10 medium plum or vine tomatoes or 1 (28-ounce) can whole peeled tomatoes, undrained
- 1 red bell pepper
- 4 jalapeños
- 1 medium red onion, chopped
- 10 garlic cloves, sliced
- ½ cup olive oil
- 1 tablespoon paprika
- 1 tablespoon chicken or vegetable bouillon powder (optional)
- 1 tablespoon sugar
- 2 teaspoons fine sea salt
- ½ teaspoon black pepper
- ½ teaspoon ground turmeric
- 2 tablespoons chopped fresh cilantro
- 2 tablespoons chopped fresh parsley

PICKLED BEET SALAD

Serves 4 to 6

I adapted this tart pickled beet dish from my aunt Rishan Mesele's recipe and find it a colorful contrast to rich foods. Rishan is one of the most adaptive cooks in our family, which stems from the many responsibilities she took on at the age of nine after her mother died.

6 medium beets
1 cup distilled white vinegar
1 cup lukewarm water
8 garlic cloves, roughly chopped
20 black peppercorns
3 bay leaves
1½ teaspoons fine sea salt

BRING A LARGE POT OF WATER to a boil. Add the beets and boil until soft and tender, about 1 hour. Peel under cold running water and cut into ½-inch cubes.

In a medium bowl, mix the vinegar, lukewarm water, garlic, peppercorns, bay leaves, and salt. Add the beets and mix well. Cover and refrigerate for a few hours to deepen the flavors before serving.

Storage The beets will keep well in the refrigerator for 3 to 4 weeks.

CRUNCHY SUNFLOWER CABBAGE SLAW

Serves 8 to 10

I created this colorful slaw to show off my favorite sunflower seed dressing. I like to serve it with Berbere Stuffed Peppers with Ground Chicken and Bulgur (page 151).

IN A LARGE BOWL, combine the red and green cabbage and sprinkle it with the salt. Squeeze the cabbage to soften it. Add the onion, jalapeño, and cilantro. Toss the dressing into the vegetables. For best results, let sit at room temperature for a few hours before serving. Squeeze fresh lime juice on top just before serving.

Storage Store covered in the fridge for up to 4 days.

4 cups shredded red cabbage

4 cups shredded green cabbage

½ teaspoon fine sea salt

1 small red onion, sliced thinly lengthwise

1 jalapeño, seeded and thinly sliced

2 tablespoons chopped fresh cilantro

Suff Dressing (page 29)

Lime wedges, for squeezing

SPRING SPINACH and WILD RAMPS

Serves 4

When a local New York farmer brought me a pile of beautiful ramps, the wild onions that sprout in the Northeast each spring, I immediately thought to pair them with korarima. This was the serendipitous, Ethiopian-influenced result.

IN A LARGE SKILLET, warm the oil over medium heat. Add the ramp bulbs and stems and sauté until softened, about 2 minutes.

Add the ramp leaves and pinches of salt and pepper and sauté until wilted, about 30 seconds. Add the spinach and more pinches of salt and pepper, cover the pan, and cook until the spinach starts to wilt, about 1 minute.

Uncover, mix in the korarima, and stir until the spinach is fully wilted, about 2 minutes. Garnish with the cashews and a squeeze of lime juice.

2 tablespoons olive oil

¼ pound ramps, bulbs and stems minced, leaves roughly cut and kept separate

Fine sea salt and black pepper

10 ounces baby spinach

⅛ teaspoon Ground Roasted Korarima (page 26)

1 teaspoon chopped cashews

Lime wedges, for squeezing

YE TIKIL GOMEN ALICHA / *CAULO*

Music-in-Your-Mouth Cabbage with Potatoes and Carrots

Serves 6 to 8

This mild stew owes its deep, satisfying flavor to a few special techniques. First, I tumble some onions into a dry pan and listen to the whisper and hiss of them dry-sautéing. Then, instead of adding the ginger and garlic at the beginning, I hold those key aromatics back until the very end so they cook just slightly from residual heat. These humble vegetables are transformed into something unique and special. Cutting the jalapeño into four long strips allows its flavor to permeate the dish without its becoming too spicy. Serve the strips to anyone who likes heat!

IN A LARGE BOWL, cover the carrots and potatoes with cold water and soak at room temperature while you prepare the other ingredients.

In a large deep pot with no oil, sauté the onions over medium heat until beginning to soften, 2 to 3 minutes. Add the oil. Drain the carrots and potatoes and add them to the pot. Cover and cook, stirring constantly, to soften the vegetables, about 5 minutes.

Stir in the turmeric, salt, and pepper. Cover and cook, stirring occasionally, until the carrots and potatoes are tender, about 5 minutes. Mix in the cabbage, cover, and cook, stirring occasionally, until the cabbage has shrunk and softened, about 15 minutes.

Stir in the garlic/ginger mixture, jalapeño, and korarima. Cover and cook, stirring occasionally, until the vegetables are soft and fragrant, 5 to 10 minutes. Taste and add salt and pepper, if necessary.

3 carrots, peeled, halved lengthwise, and sliced crosswise into half-moons ½ inch thick

2 white potatoes, peeled and cut into bite-sized pieces

2 yellow onions, sliced into thin half-moons

½ cup vegetable oil

1 teaspoon ground turmeric

¾ teaspoon fine sea salt, plus more to taste

¾ teaspoon black pepper, plus more to taste

1 head green cabbage (1½–2 pounds), cored and cut into 1-inch-wide strips

1 tablespoon ginger/garlic paste, or 2 teaspoons minced garlic plus 1 teaspoon minced fresh ginger

1 jalapeño, trimmed and cut lengthwise into four long strips (seeded if you want less heat)

½ teaspoon Ground Roasted Korarima (page 26)

MY MOTHER'S CABBAGE

Serves 10 to 12

This delicious dish combines Israeli and Moroccan influences, with a crucial dash of Ethiopian heat from the berbere. It started as something my mother whipped up after traveling from Israel to Harlem to help me with my newborn daughter in November 2005. She surveyed the ingredients I had lying around and whipped up this dish at a time when I needed comfort most. The pronounced cumin flavor gives it a distinctive scent that keeps my guests eating, and reminds me of my mother, too.

IN A LARGE POT, warm the oil over medium heat. Add the onion and sauté until softened, about 5 minutes. Add the garlic and sauté until softened, about 2 minutes.

Add the cabbage, tomatoes, bell pepper, scallions, and jalapeños and stir to combine. Mix in the berbere, cumin, salt, pepper, and half of the cilantro and stir until incorporated. Cover the pot and cook, stirring occasionally, until the vegetables have softened and released some water but the cabbage still has a gentle crunch, about 30 minutes.

Add salt and pepper to taste and serve garnished with the remaining cilantro.

½ cup vegetable oil

1 red onion, diced

6–8 garlic cloves, to taste, minced

1 head green cabbage (about 2½ pounds), quartered through the core, cored, and cut crosswise into roughly 2-inch pieces

4 tomatoes, roughly chopped, or 1 (14.5-ounce) can diced tomatoes, most of the liquid drained

1 red bell pepper, chopped

1 bunch scallions, sliced

2 jalapeños, roughly chopped, seeds included (seed if you are sensitive to heat)

2 teaspoons Berbere (page 5)

2 teaspoons ground cumin

1½ teaspoons fine sea salt, plus more to taste

1½ teaspoons black pepper, plus more to taste

1 bunch fresh cilantro, chopped

FASOLIA

Fragrant Green Beans and Carrots

Serves 6 to 8

While simple to prepare, this dish is so much better than the usual steamed green beans and carrots. It's imbued with roasted ground korarima, which lends a powerful, uniquely Ethiopian flavor.

IN A BOWL, set the carrots aside in cold water until ready to use.

In a large skillet, warm the oil over medium heat. Add the onion, ginger, garlic, and salt and sauté until the onion is softened, about 4 minutes.

Drain the carrots and add to the skillet. Cook until the carrots are softened and pliable but not cooked through, about 5 minutes.

Stir in the green beans. Cover the skillet and cook undisturbed for 5 minutes.

Uncover the pot and stir in the cumin and korarima. Sauté until the beans are dark green and blistered and the carrots are soft, adding about ½ cup water and scraping the bottom of the pan to avoid burning, 10 to 20 minutes.

Serve warm or at room temperature.

- 4 medium carrots, peeled, quartered lengthwise, and cut into 2-inch sticks
- ½ cup vegetable oil
- 1 medium red onion, halved lengthwise and sliced crosswise into thin half-moons
- 1 tablespoon minced fresh ginger
- 1 tablespoon minced garlic
- ½ teaspoon salt, plus more to taste
- 2 pounds green beans, trimmed and cut into 2- to 3-inch pieces
- 1 teaspoon ground cumin
- 1 teaspoon Ground Roasted Korarima (page 26)

BAKOLO / ILLWO

Ode to My Grandmother's Corn

Serves 4 to 6

On the Ethiopian farm where I grew up, our family's cornstalks stretched taller than me and spanned acres and acres of land. I loved to run through the cornfield, dew dripping off the corn onto my head, smelling the nearby herbs. Stepping over the peppers growing at the base of the corn, I would grab an ear and strip away the top of the husk and silk to peer at the kernels underneath. If they were small and thin, the corn was not ready—and an adult might reprimand me for stripping too early. But if they were big and fat, I knew dinner would be delicious. A few tips for the messy job of removing corn silk: I will often cut off the stem end of the corn to make this easier. You can also briefly soak the corn in water, which will make the silk come right off.

STAND THE EARS UPRIGHT on a cutting board and use a sharp knife to slice the kernels off the cobs, discarding the cobs.

In a large nonstick skillet, warm the oil over medium heat. Add the bell pepper, onion, and garlic and sauté until the onions are soft and the garlic is starting to brown, about 5 minutes.

Stir in the corn kernels, chili, cumin, salt, black pepper, and niter kibbeh and sauté until the corn is softened, about 5 minutes. Taste and add salt and pepper, if necessary.

Stir in the cilantro and scallions. Cover the pan and cook, stirring occasionally, until the corn is tender and the flavors are combined, about 5 minutes.

Ideally, cool and refrigerate for at least 2 hours so the flavors have time to integrate. However, this is also delicious served hot or at room temperature.

6 ears corn, husked and silk discarded (I always say "remove the beard")

¼ cup vegetable oil

1 red bell pepper, diced

1 small red onion, diced

6 garlic cloves, finely chopped

1 serrano pepper or jalapeño, finely chopped

½ teaspoon ground cumin

¼ teaspoon fine sea salt, plus more to taste

¼ teaspoon black pepper, plus more to taste

¼ cup Niter Kibbeh (page 15)

1 bunch fresh cilantro, leaves and stems, chopped

¼ cup chopped scallions

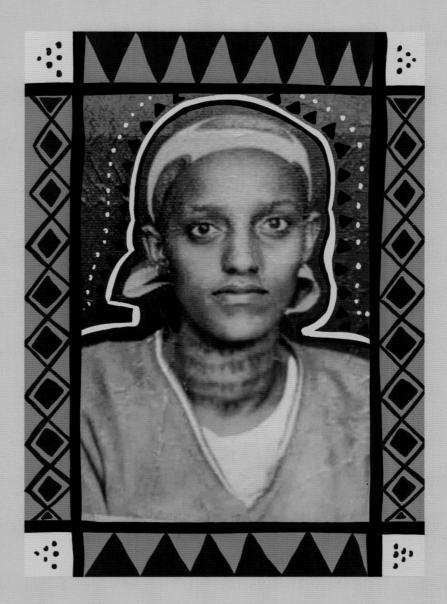

AVEJO AKLUM
An Entrepreneurial Streak

Avejo Aklum, my cousin and a sister of Ferede Aklum (page xxxi), grew up with household staff, so she never needed to work in the kitchen as a child. Her family was established and well-connected and taught Avejo and her sister to be engaged citizens. Her father had a particular soft spot for Avejo, because after she was born, the family's economic fortunes turned around.

While Ferede excelled at school and became an influential

teacher within Tigray, Avejo dropped out of school early on after other children teased her. After she was married, she had a hard time mastering cooking, to the point where her Muslim and Christian neighbors had to help her. She even had to buy injera from the store—a point of shame at the time.

But through hard work, Avejo eventually became an amazing cook. What's more, after she settled in Israel, Avejo's resourcefulness and newfound skill for cooking set her on a meaningful professional path. She now runs a business devoted to importing ingredients from Ethiopia, allowing Beta Israel families to carry on their food traditions.

Avejo was one of the very first Beta Israel to leave Tigray—all because of a letter. In 1979, her brother Ferede had been wanted by the Ethiopian government for mobilizing students. He escaped and wrote to his family, telling them he was in Sudan, headed to Israel, and encouraging them to leave as well. Word quickly spread throughout the community, and Avejo and her family had no choice but to organize and leave the country before the authorities came after them, too.

Late one night, a group of about thirty of them left Ethiopia, Avejo carrying her baby daughter, Natznet, on her back, her husband and older son, Benny, close by. While all of our journeys were treacherous, theirs was perhaps the most perilous because they only had a vague notion of where they were going, and only had time to pack minimal supplies.

Finding water was a struggle. Avejo told me her son became severely dehydrated. The group walked for miles, her son growing sicker by the hour, until her husband spotted several bees and followed them to a beehive, which was near a source of water. He dipped his fingers into the muddy water and ran them across his son's cracked lips. He tried to strain the water, but eventually they just drank muddy water, which may have saved their lives.

This journey took the Aklums three months, as they were still walking along uncertain routes. Thankfully, they received help once they crossed the border into Sudan. Avejo's mother was so well-known back in Ethiopia that when word spread that she had arrived in Sudan, she was welcomed by people who knew her and knew where Ferede was staying in Khartoum, the Sudanese capital. They were even able to send word to Ferede that his family had arrived in Sudan.

Ferede received this letter just as he was supposed to fly to

Israel, and he worried that it was a setup. Eventually, Avejo's husband managed to locate Ferede and reunite the family. Ferede was overjoyed to see all of them, and immediately brought them in for medical care.

Avejo and her family stayed only about three weeks in Sudan before flying to Greece and then to Israel. They arrived in Israel in December 1980.

Though she was thankful to have the trauma of the journey behind her, Avejo remembers that her early days in Israel were marked by a disappointment that so many of the spices and seasonings that make up the foundation of Ethiopian cooking were nowhere to be found. A friend tried to make doro wot spiced only with sweet paprika, and broke down in tears of disappointment after tasting how bland it was. Avejo's mother, who cherished the ritual of Buna—roasting her own coffee beans—suddenly could not find green coffee beans at all. The family struggled to make their injera from the only flour they could find: bleached all-purpose.

Again, the resourcefulness of Avejo and the rest of our family came into play. One of the first glimmers of hope came during a visit from Avejo's cousin Areghey Ferede, who came bearing spices, injera, and green coffee beans. He also managed to locate a slaughterhouse and buy a fresh chicken. My aunts set about thoroughly cleaning and butchering the chicken, and in the chicken's stomach, they noticed grains that they recognized: sorghum and spelt. They took them to the grocer the next day. In their then-basic Hebrew, they asked where they could buy them. "Chicken feed," not food for humans, the grocer told them dismissively.

My aunts were undeterred. They could see that the grains were unrefined, and would make much better injera than the bleached flour in the store. They simply asked other grocers until they obtained the grains they wanted. They took them to a mill and had them ground into flour. They brought the flour home to the trailer park in Be'er Sheva, where they were living, and made the best injera they had made since coming to Israel. Avejo remembered that her mother was particularly joyful, dashing through the trailer park sharing the good news, and the community rejoiced right along with her, knowing this was a watershed moment that would make Israel feel much more like home.

AVEJO'S DISHES

Avejo and her husband bought more of the grain, took it to a mill, and began distributing it to their fellow Beta Israel. And this was the start of their very own business. It began with a store, then eventually they built their own mill where they could make flour from any type of grain.

Avejo and her husband could see that there was clearly a need to provide Ethiopian ingredients for the Beta Israel community who had immigrated to Israel. They worked hard to source teff, but the quality was unacceptable. They were unable to import high-quality teff until the 1990s.

Now they have a thriving business that specializes in selling grains, lentils, chickpeas, and spices that are in demand among Ethiopians living in Israel. I am so proud of Auntie Avejo and how she overcame so much to become a successful international businesswoman who brings a bit of home to our community.

ALICHA WOT / *ALICHA TSEBHI*

Mild Vegetable Stew

Serves 4 to 6

Traditionally, Ethiopian vegetable stew is based around cabbage, carrots, and potatoes, but my cousin Avejo Aklum (page 101) swaps the cabbage for zucchini, and adds just a bit of heat from berbere for her signature stew: I've adapted her method here.

IN A DRY MEDIUM POT, sauté the onion over low heat for 3 minutes. Add the garlic and cook until the onion is translucent, 5 to 10 minutes.

Stir in the potatoes, carrots, jalapeño, hot water, oil, bouillon powder, turmeric, paprika, salt, black pepper, korarima, and cumin. Cover and cook, stirring occasionally, just until the potatoes are tender, about 15 minutes.

Add the zucchini and simmer just until tender, 5 to 10 minutes. Taste and add salt, if necessary. Serve over injera.

- 1 medium red onion, chopped
- 6 garlic cloves, minced
- 5 medium russet potatoes, peeled and cut into 1-inch chunks
- 3 large carrots, peeled and diced
- 1 jalapeño or serrano pepper, roughly chopped, with seeds
- ½ cup hot water
- ⅓ cup olive oil
- 1 tablespoon chicken or vegetable bouillon powder
- 1 teaspoon ground turmeric
- 1 teaspoon sweet paprika
- 2 teaspoons fine sea salt, plus more to taste
- 1 teaspoon black pepper
- ½ teaspoon Ground Roasted Korarima (page 26)
- ½ teaspoon ground cumin
- 3 medium zucchini, peeled and cut into 1-inch chunks
- Injera (page 37), for serving

GOMEN / HAMLI

Braised Collard Greens

Serves 4 as a main dish, 6 to 8 as a side dish

Gomen makes me think of my grandmother. She used to grow a very soft, delicate type of wild greens in Ethiopia, and was delighted to find a similar green while foraging after we settled in Israel. This dish of mellow greens is a traditional accompaniment to Doro Wot (page 143), the collards providing a nice foil for the rich, spicy stew. Collard greens are also a common dish among non-Ethiopian Jewish cooks and are typically accessible and inexpensive.

1 cup vegetable oil

1 red onion, diced

2 teaspoons minced garlic

1 teaspoon minced fresh ginger

2 pounds collard greens, washed well, thick bottom stems cut off, leaves rolled into cylinders and finely chopped

1½ teaspoons fine sea salt, plus more to taste

½ teaspoon black pepper, plus more to taste

¼ teaspoon ground nutmeg

1 jalapeño, cut lengthwise into four long pieces

IN A MEDIUM POT, warm the oil over medium heat. Add the onion and sauté, stirring occasionally, until softened, about 5 minutes. Add the garlic and ginger and sauté until lightly browned and fragrant, about 10 minutes.

Add the collard greens, salt, and pepper. Cook uncovered, stirring occasionally, until the greens are dark green and tender, about 30 minutes. If greens start to scorch, add water, a few tablespoons at a time.

Taste and add salt and pepper, if necessary. Stir in the nutmeg and the jalapeño slices.

QEY SIR / QEYH SUR

Braised Beets

Serves 10 to 12

I love everything about beets: How their vibrant purple color complements the rainbow of other stews on the Ethiopian table. How simple to prepare but delicious they are. And especially how the Hebrew word for beet, *selek*, has the same root word as the phrase for "driven out of something," so when we place beets on the celebratory Rosh Hashanah table, it's symbolic of starting fresh. This is good hot, cold, or at room temperature, making it a terrific food to leave out at a long party when you'd rather be socializing. Feel free to alter the size of the beets and the onions to your liking. Wear gloves if you don't want pink hands!

6 beets, washed and trimmed

⅓ cup vegetable oil

1 yellow onion, diced

2 teaspoons minced garlic

1 teaspoon minced fresh ginger

½ teaspoon ground cumin

¼ teaspoon fine sea salt, plus more to taste

¼ teaspoon black pepper, plus more to taste

¼ bunch fresh cilantro, leaves and tender stems, chopped

1 jalapeño (optional), with or without seeds, chopped

IN A LARGE POT, combine the beets with water to cover. Bring to a boil and cook until tender, 45 minutes to 1 hour. Drain the beets and let cool slightly. Peel and cut into bite-sized cubes.

Meanwhile, in a large wide pot or deep sauté pan, heat the oil, onion, garlic, and ginger over medium heat. Stir, lowering the heat if the onion begins to brown, until softened and fragrant, about 5 minutes. (Don't turn up the heat: You want the onion soft, not jumpy and cranky.)

Stir in the beets, cumin, salt, pepper, cilantro, and jalapeño (if using). Cover and cook for about 5 minutes to let the flavors integrate. Taste and add salt and pepper, if necessary.

INIGUDAYI TIBS / *KANTISHALA TIBSI*

Sautéed Mushrooms with Rosemary

Serves 4

I regard mushrooms as a beautiful treat from nature. In March/April and September/October each year, they grew wild in the forested, hilly area near where I grew up in Tigray, and I remember creeping through the trees, peering at the ground for the dark, rounded mushrooms sprouting from the ground, before making this quick and delicious dish, which is rich from the butter and zippy from the spices. I now use purchased Baby Bella mushrooms—you can use any sliced mushroom you'd like—but this dish still evokes the thrill of foraging as a child.

WARM A LARGE DRY SKILLET over medium heat. Add the onion and sauté until slightly softened, 1 to 2 minutes. Stir in the mushrooms, red wine, 1 tablespoon of the niter kibbeh, the rosemary, jalapeño (if using), garlic, ginger, berbere, awaze, salt, and pepper and sauté, adding 1 tablespoon more wine at a time if the mixture starts to stick to the bottom of the pan, until the mushrooms are softened, about 10 minutes.

Stir in the tomato, the remaining 1 tablespoon niter kibbeh, and the korarima and sauté for 5 more minutes. Serve immediately.

- 1 red onion, sliced into half-moons
- 8 ounces Baby Bella or any other mushrooms, wiped clean and sliced
- 1 cup red wine, plus more if necessary
- 2 tablespoons Niter Kibbeh (page 15)
- 1 sprig fresh rosemary
- 1 large jalapeño (optional), sliced into thick rings
- ¾ teaspoon minced garlic
- ¼ teaspoon minced fresh ginger
- 1 teaspoon Berbere (page 5)
- 1 teaspoon Awaze (page 32)
- ½ teaspoon fine sea salt
- ½ teaspoon black pepper
- 1 tomato, cut into bite-sized pieces
- 1 teaspoon Ground Roasted Korarima (page 26)

BAMYA

Okra Stew with Tomatoes

Serves 4

I ate a lot of okra stews over rice during the period of my childhood that my family spent in Sudan. I wanted to pay tribute to that time by creating an okra stew that had none of the slimy, mushy texture that I remember from childhood. I cut the okra into chunks and cook just until tender. This stew is an ideal use for soft, overripe tomatoes, which meld easily into the okra. It is delicious served over rice or injera.

IN A LARGE POT, heat the oil over medium heat. Add the onion and garlic and sauté until the onions are translucent and the garlic is beginning to brown, about 5 minutes.

Stir in the berbere and cumin and stir to integrate. Add the tomatoes and cook, stirring occasionally, until they break down into a saucy consistency, adding up to 1½ cups of water if they start to stick to the bottom of the pot, 10 to 12 minutes.

Mix in the okra, salt, and pepper, reduce the heat to medium-low, cover the pot, and simmer, stirring occasionally and adding more water as needed to keep the tomatoes from sticking to the bottom of the pot, until the okra is tender and starting to split, 10 to 15 minutes.

Stir in the korarima and simmer to blend the flavors, about 5 minutes.

Serve with injera or rice.

½ cup vegetable oil

1 small red onion, diced

6 garlic cloves, chopped

1½ teaspoons Berbere (page 5)

1 teaspoon ground cumin

3 tomatoes, diced

1 pound okra, trimmed and cut into 1-inch pieces

½ teaspoon fine sea salt, plus more to taste

½ teaspoon black pepper, plus more to taste

¼ teaspoon Ground Roasted Korarima (page 26), ground cardamom, or more cumin

Injera (page 37) or rice, for serving

DUBBA WOT / DUBBA TSEBHI

Pumpkin Stew with Date Honey

Serves 8

Ethiopian and Israeli cooking traditions come together in this vegetarian stew adapted from my aunt Genet (Ilana) Mamay's family recipe, with the addition of silan, a date honey that is often used as a natural sweetener. When Genet was growing up in Ethiopia, dates were considered candy, and anything sweet was rarely consumed. However, upon moving to Israel, where people's palates are more used to sugar, her family found that the silan cuts the spice: The more you add, the less spicy the stew will be.

IN A LARGE DRY POT, sauté the onion over medium heat, stirring constantly, until translucent, about 3 minutes. Add the oil, tomato paste, garlic, ginger, and ½ cup of the hot water and bring to a simmer. Stir in the delleh, silan, salt, pepper, and korarima and stir well to incorporate, about 1 minute.

Stir in the squash and remaining 5½ cups hot water. Reduce the heat to low, cover, and cook, stirring occasionally, until the pumpkin is tender, about 25 minutes.

Serve on top of injera.

1 medium red onion, chopped

½ cup olive oil

1 (6-ounce) can tomato paste

1 tablespoon plus 1 teaspoon minced garlic

2 teaspoons minced fresh ginger

6 cups (1,440 grams) hot water

2 tablespoons Delleh (page 11) or Berbere (page 5)

1–2 tablespoons silan (date honey), to taste (depending on how sweet you'd like your stew)

2 teaspoons fine sea salt

1 teaspoon black pepper

½ teaspoon Ground Roasted Korarima (page 26)

4 pounds kabocha or calabaza squash (these are often labeled as Japanese pumpkin or West Indian pumpkin) or butternut squash, peeled and cut into ½-inch cubes

Injera (page 37), for serving

DINICHE ALICHA / *DINISH ALICHA*

Red Potato Stew with Turmeric and Jalapeño

Serves 6 to 8

This is a simple, delicately flavored potato stew that goes nicely with nonspicy meat dishes, such as Doro Wot Alicha (page 145). Here again, we use the method of cooking onions in a dry pot before softening them in oil, which concentrates the onion flavor. When dry-sautéing, it's important to stir frequently to avoid sticking or burning, and to reduce the heat when necessary. Adding the jalapeño at the end infuses just a bit of heat into the stew.

IN A DRY MEDIUM DUTCH OVEN or heavy-bottomed pot, stir the onions over medium heat. When they start to sizzle, after about 3 minutes, add the oil and sauté, stirring frequently, until the onions soften, 6 to 8 minutes. Stir in the garlic, ginger, and turmeric and cook, stirring occasionally, until the mixture is bright yellow, about 5 minutes.

Add the potatoes, carrots, salt, pepper, and ½ cup water. Cover the pot and cook, stirring frequently, until the potatoes are tender, 15 to 20 minutes, adding up to ½ cup more water to loosen anything stuck to the bottom of the pot.

Stir in the jalapeño, cover, and cook, stirring occasionally, to infuse the flavors, about 5 minutes. Taste and add salt and pepper, if necessary.

- 1 large or 2 small yellow onions, halved and thinly sliced
- ½ cup vegetable oil
- 2 teaspoons minced garlic
- 1 teaspoon minced fresh ginger
- 1 teaspoon ground turmeric
- 2 pounds red potatoes (about 9), unpeeled and cut into 1-inch cubes
- 1 pound carrots (about 2 large), peeled and cut on the bias into ½-inch-thick slices
- 1½ teaspoons fine sea salt, plus more to taste
- ½ teaspoon black pepper, plus more to taste
- 1 large jalapeño, quartered lengthwise

TSION CAFÉ'S SHAKSHUKA

Poached Eggs in Tomato Sauce

Serves 4 to 6

This easy dish, well-known throughout the Middle East and North Africa, is one of the best-known dishes at Tsion Café, and has even been featured on the *Today* show. It's also what I have long made when I'm hungry, but not in the mood to do any major cooking. As a single woman in my twenties, living alone in Harlem, often arriving home from work late at night and finding a near-bare refrigerator, I found that shakshuka was a savior: It could be made with ingredients that I kept on hand, I could experiment with different spice levels and a variety of vegetables, and it was inexpensive and filling, especially served alongside pitas or injera. Though many American restaurants are now serving shakshuka for brunch, mine is unique: The berbere gives it a sultry kick that keeps my customers coming back.

½ cup vegetable oil

1 yellow onion, diced

6 garlic cloves, minced

1 small or ½ large red bell pepper, diced

1 small or ½ large green bell pepper, diced

1 (28-ounce) can diced tomatoes, undrained

½ jalapeño (optional, for more heat)

1–1½ teaspoons Berbere (page 5), to taste

1 teaspoon ground cumin

1 teaspoon ground paprika

¾ teaspoon fine sea salt, plus more to taste

¼ teaspoon black pepper

½ bunch fresh cilantro, leaves and thin stems, chopped

4–6 large eggs

1 tablespoon crumbled feta cheese (preferably made with Israeli goat's milk)

IN A MEDIUM CAST-IRON SKILLET, warm the oil over medium-low heat. Add the onion and garlic and sauté until soft, about 10 minutes. Add the red and green bell peppers and sauté until soft, about 10 minutes.

Add the tomatoes and their juices, the jalapeño (if using), berbere, cumin, paprika, salt, and black pepper. Simmer, stirring occasionally, until the tomatoes have broken down and are fully combined with the bell peppers, about 15 minutes.

Add the cilantro (reserving a tablespoon for garnish) and stir. Taste and adjust the salt and spice levels.

Increase the heat to medium. Using a spoon, make 4 to 6 wells in the tomatoes. Add 1 egg to each well. Cook uncovered until the egg whites become cloudy, 2 to 3 minutes. Cover the pan and cook until the yolks are runny (about 4 minutes) or firm (about 6 minutes), depending on your preference. (Use your fingertip to gently nudge the yolk to gauge its firmness. When it jumps back at you, it's runny.)

Remove from the heat. Garnish with the reserved chopped cilantro and the feta cheese.

CHAPTER 5

LEGUMES AND GRAINS

Legumes and grains form the basis for many Ethiopian diets and are a cherished part of my family's meals. In her final hours, my grandmother wished for just one dish: a simple stew of black-eyed peas and barley (see page 125). Her niece Aster Solomon (page 59) warmly remembers raw yellow chickpeas as a favorite from growing up on her family's Ethiopian farm. And once our family began to integrate into Israel, another cousin, Mali Aklum, looked forward to blending chickpeas into hummus with her mother, Samira, and drizzling it with a bright-red stew base.

I invite you to make these delicious dishes part of your family traditions, too.

BLACK-EYED PEAS and BARLEY SALAD with ARUGULA

Serves 4 as a side dish

Black-eyed peas and barley are a comforting, nutritious combination, and in fact were my grandmother's last request (see My Grandmother's Black-Eyed Peas and Barley Stew, page 125). I developed this salad to show the versatility of these ingredients: You can make a hearty stew, like that one, or a refreshing salad, like this.

5 ounces dried black-eyed peas

2 teaspoons fine sea salt

½ cup hulled barley (see Note)

10 ounces cherry or grape tomatoes, halved

3–4 cups arugula or mixed greens

½ cup Suff Dressing (page 29), plus more to taste

IN A MEDIUM POT, combine the peas with water to cover and 1 teaspoon of the salt. Bring to a boil over medium heat and cook until tender, about 55 minutes. Drain and cool before using.

Meanwhile, in another medium pot, combine the barley with water to cover and the remaining 1 teaspoon salt. Bring to a boil over medium heat and cook until tender, about 55 minutes, adding a little more water if the pan begins to dry out. Drain and cool before using.

In a bowl, toss the peas and barley with the tomatoes, arugula, and ½ cup dressing. Taste and add additional dressing, if desired.

Note If using pearl barley, cook according to the package directions. The cooking time will be shorter than that given for hulled barley.

SHIWAYNISH TZGAI

"My Sweetie"

My special name for Shiwaynish, my mother's sister, is Maa-Ray, which means "my honey," or "my sweetie."

Unlike most Ethiopian women, Shiwaynish didn't cook much when she was growing up, and had comparatively few responsibilities. She was lucky enough to have two older sisters (one of whom was my mother) who were often at work in the kitchen while she immersed herself in fashion, dancing, and

SHIWAYNISH'S DISHES

socializing into her teens. So many of her memories are joyful and carefree. She recalls celebrating the Ethiopian New Year by giving out daisies, exchanging gifts, dancing outside with the neighbors, and eating delicious food. She remembers visiting the village market as the new year approached one year, and coveting a unique, fashionable dress—which her family refused to buy her. So Shiwaynish, in turn, refused to eat or talk to anyone. (She did eventually get another dress that she wanted.)

Once she got married, she learned all about cooking traditional Ethiopian foods from her mother-in-law. While she got a late start, Shiwaynish now boasts that eventually she was making food so well that her mother-in-law would choose to come to Shiwaynish's house to eat, rather than cooking her own food.

When her father died, Shiwaynish was still a toddler. This left my grandmother Bezabish Worku, affectionately known as Babish, to raise six kids on her own with no help. In addition to raising Shiwaynish, my mother, and their siblings, she raised her nieces and nephews after the death of her brother, *and* she played a large part in raising me as well. Once we immigrated to Israel, her house became the place where everyone gathered, ate, and celebrated.

My aunt has loving memories of my grandmother throughout her life, but she also has particularly significant memories of her when she was dying. When Babish became sick, Shiwaynish took her to her house, where she made Hanza (page 64) and porridge for her. In her last days, Babish asked for Black-Eyed Peas and Barley Stew (page 125), and lovingly said goodbye to our family. My aunt recalls that my grandmother was very spiritual, and didn't suffer or agonize over her impending death. She just knew it was her time to leave. We called her a Tsadik in Hebrew: a righteous person, who does not suffer and has an easy transition to death.

Shiwaynish told me that food—in this case fruit—played a similar role in the death of her own sister Tekavesh, who died of cancer several years later. On a rainy day just before she died, Tekavesh asked Shiwaynish to bring her a particular type of local fruit, which Shiwaynish did. It would be the last time they talked. This, to me, shows the power of food to comfort and alleviate suffering in a person's final days.

MY GRAND-MOTHER'S BLACK-EYED PEAS and BARLEY STEW

Serves 4

Simple, nutritious, wholesome, comforting, and gently spiced with Ethiopian flavors: My grandmother requested this for her last meal before she died.

10 ounces dried black-eyed peas
3 teaspoons fine sea salt
½ cup hulled barley (see Note)
¼ cup olive oil
1 small red onion, chopped
¼ cup Kulet (page 6)
1 tablespoon Ayib (page 18)
1 teaspoon Niter Kibbeh (page 15), melted
Cooked rice (optional), for serving

IN A MEDIUM POT, combine the peas, water to cover, and 1 teaspoon of the salt. Bring to a boil over medium heat and cook until tender, about 55 minutes. Drain the peas.

Meanwhile, in another medium pot, combine the barley, water to cover, and 1 teaspoon of the salt. Bring to a boil over medium heat and cook until tender, about 55 minutes, adding a little more water if the pot becomes dry. Drain the barley.

In a medium pot, warm the oil over medium heat. Add the onion and sauté until softened, about 5 minutes. Add the kulet and stir, then add the cooked peas, barley, the remaining 1 teaspoon salt, and 1 cup water and simmer uncovered, stirring occasionally, until most of the water is absorbed and the mixture is a thick stew, about 15 minutes, adding up to 1 cup additional water if the mixture starts to look dry.

Taste and adjust the salt, if necessary. Garnish with the ayib and niter kibbeh. Serve with rice, if desired.

Note If using pearl barley, cook according to the package directions. The cooking time will be shorter than that given for hulled barley.

AZIFA SALAD

Refreshing Lentil Salad

Serves 8 to 10

As a child, I remember eating many cool lentil salads like this one. Not only are they an ideal dish for warm weather, their light, nutritious nature makes them perfect for breaking fasts.

IN A LARGE POT, combine the lentils, oil, and 4 cups water. Bring to a boil over medium heat and cook until the lentils are tender, about 30 minutes. Drain the lentils, spread onto a large tray or plate, and cool to room temperature.

Meanwhile, in a large bowl, mix the onion with the lime juice and let sit for at least 10 minutes.

Add the cooled lentils, cilantro, jalapeño, mustard, cumin, salt, and black pepper and stir to combine. Taste and add more lime juice, salt, or pepper, if necessary. Garnish with the remaining cilantro.

Refrigerate for at least 20 minutes to allow the flavors to blend together. Serve chilled or at room temperature, with any of the garnishes you like.

2 cups brown or green lentils, rinsed

1 tablespoon vegetable oil

1 red onion, finely diced

Juice of 1 lime or lemon, plus more to taste

½ bunch fresh cilantro, leaves and tender stems, finely chopped, plus more for garnish

1 large jalapeño, minced

¼ cup Senafich (page 30) or Dijon mustard

½ teaspoon ground cumin

½ teaspoon fine sea salt, plus more to taste

¼ teaspoon black pepper, plus more to taste

OPTIONAL GARNISHES

Chopped tomatoes

Chopped bell pepper

Ayib (page 18)

Injera Chips (page 43)

SHIRO
Silky Chickpea Stew

Serves 4

Shiro—a stew of chickpeas, garlic, ginger, and berbere—is a beloved hallmark of Ethiopian cuisine. The most common way to make it is from shiro powder, a dried mix of chickpea flour and spices, which is quick, convenient and—for my fellow refugees and me—meaningful and life-sustaining. My relatives carried a supply of shiro powder on the road through Sudan, and whenever they needed a meal, they simply added water and cooked it over a fire. Many Beta Israel abstain from dairy and milk on Wednesdays and Fridays, and turn to this staple. Shiro powder is available at Ethiopian stores and online: Note that each brand has its own seasoning, which is convenient, but also means that you have less control over the flavor. See Beejhy's Shiro (page 131) for a variation that uses canned chickpeas instead of powder.

½ cup vegetable oil

2 teaspoons minced garlic

1 teaspoon minced fresh ginger

1 cup shiro powder

½ teaspoon fine sea salt,
   plus more to taste

½ teaspoon black pepper,
   plus more to taste

¼ teaspoon ground cumin
   (optional)

IN A MEDIUM POT, warm the oil over medium heat. Add the garlic and ginger, mix for about 1 minute, then add 2⅔ cups water and whisk well until thoroughly combined, about 2 minutes.

Add the shiro powder, salt, pepper, and cumin (if using). Whisk vigorously to smooth the mixture and simmer, stirring constantly, until it is very thick, 8 to 10 minutes. Taste and add salt and pepper, if necessary.

MESSER WOT / BIRSEN TSEBHI

Slow-Cooked Red Lentil Stew

Serves 6 to 8

The appeal of lentil stew goes back to Biblical times, when Esau lost his birthright over a bowl of it. Today, we Beta Israel consider it fundamental to every meal. While red lentils cook much more quickly than other types, taking our time helps them develop the right flavor and texture. This recipe makes a medium-spiced stew; feel free to add more berbere.

IN A FOOD PROCESSOR, process the onions, garlic, and ginger into a thick paste. Pour into a large pot and bring to a simmer over medium heat. Cook, stirring occasionally, until most of the liquid has evaporated, 5 to 10 minutes.

Add the oil and simmer for another 10 minutes. Stir in the berbere, salt, and pepper. Simmer, stirring and scraping constantly, until the stew is deep red and thickened and the onions are melting into each other, 15 to 20 minutes, adding a few tablespoons of water to help loosen anything sticking to the bottom of the pot, and adding a few tablespoons more oil if the mixture begins to look dry.

Add the tomato paste. Fill half of the empty tomato paste can with water, scrape the remaining paste off the sides of the can into the water, and pour that into the pot. Bring to a boil and simmer until the tomato paste melts into the base, 15 to 20 minutes, adding up to another cup of water to help integrate the two if necessary.

Stir in the lentils and 4 cups water, return to a simmer, and cook for 10 minutes. Add 1 cup water and cook until the lentils begin to disintegrate into the stew, about 10 minutes longer. Stir in the korarima. Taste and add salt and pepper, if necessary. Serve warm.

4 medium red onions, quartered, soaked briefly in water (to reduce the astringency), and drained

1 tablespoon minced garlic

1 tablespoon minced fresh ginger

¾ cup vegetable oil, plus more as needed

3 tablespoons Berbere (page 5)

1½ teaspoons fine sea salt, plus more to taste

1½ teaspoons black pepper, plus more to taste

1 (6-ounce) can tomato paste

3 cups red lentils, rinsed well

1 teaspoon Ground Roasted Korarima (page 26) or ground cardamom

BEEJHY'S SHIRO

Serves 10 to 12

When I first moved to the United States, shiro powder was nearly impossible to find. Going without this beautiful, nutritious chickpea stew was simply not an option for me: Its smooth texture was something I longed for at every family meal. So I developed my own version that uses canned chickpeas, blended in a food processor, but that still captures all the silkiness of the original. It takes longer to come together than shiro made with the powder (see page 127), but the food processor does most of the work.

IN A FOOD PROCESSOR, process the onions, ginger, and garlic to make a thick paste.

Pour into a large pot, bring to a simmer over medium heat, and cook until most of the water has evaporated, 5 to 10 minutes.

Stir in the oil and simmer for another 10 minutes. Stir in the berbere, 2 teaspoons of the salt, and 1½ teaspoons of the pepper. Simmer, stirring and scraping constantly, until the mixture is deep red and thickened and the onions are melting into each other, 15 to 20 minutes, adding a few tablespoons of water to help loosen anything sticking to the bottom of the pot.

Add the tomato paste. Fill half of the empty tomato paste can with water, scrape the remaining paste off the sides of the can into the water, and pour that into the pot. Bring to a boil and simmer until the tomato paste melts into the base, adding up to another cup of water to help integrate the two if necessary, 15 to 20 minutes.

Meanwhile, in a clean food processor bowl, blend the chickpeas and their liquid until smooth and creamy, about 5 minutes. You cannot overblend the chickpeas, so take your time!

Pour the chickpeas into the pot. Add the remaining ½ teaspoon salt and ½ teaspoon pepper. Bring to a simmer and cook, stirring frequently and adding water if necessary, until the mixture is creamy and silky, 25 to 30 minutes. Taste and add salt and pepper, if necessary. Serve warm.

4 medium red onions, quartered, soaked briefly in water (to reduce the astringency), and drained

1 tablespoon minced fresh ginger (about a 1½-inch piece ginger)

1 tablespoon minced garlic (about 4 cloves)

¾ cup vegetable oil

3 tablespoons Berbere (page 5)

2½ teaspoons fine sea salt, plus more to taste

2 teaspoons black pepper, plus more to taste

1 (6-ounce) can tomato paste

4 (15.5-ounce) cans chickpeas, undrained

KIK ALICHA / *ATER ALICAH*

Sunny Yellow Split Pea Stew

Serves 6 to 8

This mild stew is so versatile—you can spread it on bread, use it as a dip for crudités or injera chips, dollop it on a salad, or just serve it as part of a bountiful Ethiopian spread. It shows how melting onions can add stock-like flavor to stews. It also freezes and reheats well, so feel free to double the recipe.

IN A BOWL, soak the split peas in cold water for 5 to 10 minutes and pick them over. Wash several times until the water is only mildly cloudy. (If you want to quicken the cooking, soak the split peas for 30 minutes to 1 hour; do not soak overnight.)

In a large dry pot, cook the onions, garlic, and ginger over medium heat, stirring gently, until the water mostly evaporates and the mixture looks dry, about 5 minutes.

Stir in the oil and cook, stirring occasionally, for 5 minutes. Stir in the salt, pepper, and turmeric. Stir in the split peas and 5 cups water, cover, and simmer, stirring about every 5 minutes, until the peas are soft and the stew is thick and saucy, about 45 minutes.

Stir in the jalapeño. Serve over injera or with rice.

2 cups dried yellow split peas

2 yellow onions, very finely chopped (or roughly chopped and then blended in a food processor)

2 teaspoons minced garlic

1 teaspoon minced fresh ginger

½ cup vegetable oil

2 teaspoons fine sea salt, plus more to taste

2 teaspoons black pepper, plus more to taste

1 teaspoon ground turmeric

1 jalapeño, halved lengthwise and seeded

Injera (page 37) or cooked rice, for serving

AVEJO'S TIMTIMO

Mild Fava and Yellow Split Pea Stew

Serves 4 to 6

Kik Alicha (page 132) is typically made with just one type of bean, but that was too simple for my aunt Avejo Aklum (page 101). This is her unique blend of fava beans and yellow split peas. The two delicious flavors complement each other beautifully, and blending them together results in a silky, creamy mixture that rivals even Shiro (page 127).

IN A MEDIUM POT, combine the fava beans and split peas and add water to cover by 1 to 2 inches. Bring to a boil over medium-high heat. Skim off any foam on the surface, reduce the heat to maintain a simmer, and cook until tender, 30 to 40 minutes.

Place a strainer over a bowl. Drain the beans and reserve the bean water. Let both cool slightly. Rinse and dry the pot.

In a food processor, blend the onions, garlic, and ginger until they form a paste. Pour into the pot and cook over medium heat, stirring constantly, for 5 minutes. Add the salt and pepper and continue cooking until the water evaporates from the mixture, about 3 minutes.

Stir in the olive oil, delleh, and hot water. Bring to a boil, cover the pot, and cook, stirring occasionally, until the sauce comes together, 10 to 12 minutes.

Meanwhile, add the cooked beans and 2 cups bean water to the food processor and blend until smooth and creamy, adding up to 1 cup more water if necessary, about 2 minutes.

Mix the bean puree into the pot, add the korarima, reduce the heat to low, and cook for 5 minutes to blend the flavors.

Serve on top of injera.

2 cups dried split fava beans, well rinsed

1 cup dried yellow split peas, well rinsed

2 medium red onions, diced

6 garlic cloves, minced

1 tablespoon grated fresh ginger

1½ teaspoons salt

½ teaspoon black pepper

½ cup olive oil

2 tablespoons Delleh (page 11) or Berbere (page 5)

1 cup hot water

¼ teaspoon Ground Roasted Korarima (page 26)

Injera (page 37), for serving

SAMBUSA

Savory Fried Lentil Pockets

Makes 12 sambusa

This fried snack and appetizer, popular throughout Africa and the Middle East, is one of my favorite ways to use up leftover cooked lentils or stew. Here I've made it simple by using a tortilla instead of a dough. Feel free to double or triple the recipe for more guests: These go fast!

1 cup cooked brown or green lentils, at room temperature

¼ red onion, finely diced

½ jalapeño (optional, for heat), chopped

Fine sea salt

Squeeze of lemon juice (optional)

2 tablespoons all-purpose flour

2 (12-inch) flour tortillas, each cut into 6 equal wedges

Vegetable oil, for frying

Awaze (page 32; optional), for dipping

IN A MEDIUM BOWL, mix together the lentils, onion, jalapeño, salt to taste, and lemon juice (if using). Set aside.

In a small bowl, mix the flour and 2 tablespoons water into a paste, mixing in more water, 1 teaspoon at a time, if necessary.

Microwave the tortilla wedges for just 15 seconds to soften, then immediately transfer all but one wedge into a container to keep soft.

Place the one tortilla wedge on a work surface with the point facing away from you. Take the two corners of the wedge that are closest to you and fold them inward to meet in the middle. Dab a bit of the flour-water mixture to seal those folded edges together into a cone shape. Hold the cone in your hand with the point of the wedge facing up and fill the opening with a heaping tablespoon of lentil filling. Brush the flour-water mixture along the edges of the pointed tip, fold that tip down over the cone to create a triangle shape, and gently press the edges to seal them in place. Repeat with the remaining tortilla wedges and filling and set aside.

In a large cast-iron skillet, heat about ½ inch of oil over high heat until it reaches about 350°F on a deep-fry thermometer (or when a tiny pinch of flour sizzles when added to the oil). Working in batches, add the sambusa to the hot oil and fry, flipping once, until deep golden brown, 2 to 3 minutes per side.

Serve with the awaze as a dipping sauce, if desired.

HUMMUS with SPICY SILSI

Serves about 8

The inspiration for this hummus came from Mali Aklum, the daughter of Ferede Aklum (page xxxi), who heroically brought so many Ethiopian Jewish families to Israel. It combines the hummus that our family learned to make in our new home of Israel with the fiery flavors of Ethiopia. Mali remembers it as a special treat that she and her mother enjoyed after a long day of cooking Spicy Chicken Drumstick Stew (page 143). It's an excellent way to use up any leftover kulet, the base for many of my stews.

IN A FOOD PROCESSOR, combine the chickpeas, garlic, lemon juice, tahini, berbere, salt, and pepper. Blend until smooth, adding about 3 tablespoons of the chickpea liquid, 1 tablespoon at a time, to help blend into a smooth, creamy, airy mixture, about 3 minutes.

Transfer the hummus to a large shallow serving bowl. Smooth it out so that it is higher on the sides, with a divot in the center. Spoon the kulet into the middle. Garnish with the eggs (if using), and serve cold or at room temperature with injera chips, pita slices, or pita chips for scooping.

2 (15.5-ounce) cans chickpeas, liquid drained and reserved

3 large garlic cloves, roughly chopped

Juice of 1 lemon (3–4 tablespoons)

2 tablespoons well-mixed tahini

½ teaspoon Berbere (page 5)

½ teaspoon fine sea salt

¼ teaspoon black pepper

1 cup cold or room temperature Kulet (page 6)

2 boiled eggs (optional), quartered, for garnish

Injera Chips (page 43) or pita slices or chips, for serving

TSION CAFÉ'S JOLLOF RICE

Serves 8

After an employee from Nigeria taught me to cook his favorite version of this classic West African rice dish, I immediately added it to the menu of Tsion Café. I love how the dish shows the diversity of the African diaspora, and how adding berbere infuses it with Ethiopian flavor. It quickly became a bestseller, and many customers have told me they come to us specifically to try it. During the pandemic, we made enormous pots of this rice, selling it as takeout and also donating thousands of portions to the hungry. People were looking for comfort, and we were happy to provide it: Our work was even featured on the *Today* show. The key to this dish is to let it cook undisturbed so that you get a crunchy dark crust on the bottom, which will infuse the rice with a gently smoky flavor.

IN A FOOD PROCESSOR, blend the tomatoes, carrots, onions, jalapeños, garlic, and ginger into a rough puree. (You may need to do this in 2 batches.) Pour the mixture into a large pot. Add about ½ cup water to the food processor to wash out any puree stuck to the sides and add to the pot.

Place the pot over medium heat and cook, stirring occasionally to prevent sticking on the bottom and sides of the pot, until the water has mostly evaporated, about 25 minutes: It should bubble up through the vegetables but not pool on the bottom of the pot.

Stir in the oil and simmer until fully integrated, about 30 minutes: It should pool in the vegetables but not on the bottom of the pan.

Stir in the berbere, bouillon powder, salt, black pepper, curry powder, and thyme and cook for about 5 minutes to integrate the flavors.

Rinse the rice once, then immediately mix into the sauce. Reduce the heat to medium-low, cover the pot, and cook undisturbed for 5 minutes.

Mix in 1 cup water, cover the pot, and cook undisturbed until the rice is tender and a dark, crispy layer has formed on the bottom, about 20 minutes. You may see smoke rising from underneath the lid; this is desirable! Serve warm.

4 plum tomatoes, cut into about 8 pieces each

3 large carrots, peeled and cut into chunks

2 large yellow onions, cut into about 8 pieces each

2 large jalapeños, quartered lengthwise

6 garlic cloves, peeled but whole

3" chunk fresh ginger, peeled and roughly chopped

1 cup vegetable oil

1 tablespoon Berbere (page 5)

1 tablespoon chicken or vegetable bouillon powder

1½ teaspoons fine sea salt

1½ teaspoons black pepper

1 teaspoon curry powder

¼ teaspoon dried thyme

3 cups parboiled long-grained rice (I use Ben's Original)

CHAPTER 6

MEAT AND FISH

When I was growing up, the vast majority of our meals were made mostly with vegetables and grains. Meat was strictly reserved for special occasions, often Shabbat, celebrations, or holidays. Freshly butchered chickens were carefully and thoroughly washed to adhere to Jewish law, which prohibits consuming blood. Then they were butchered in twelve pieces, the meatiest parts given to honored guests, and the rest dispersed among the family. When a cow was butchered, the meat would be spread among several families, much of it for use in fragrant stews.

This chapter provides the foundation for these celebratory meat stews. It also explores options for fish dishes, which I often eat on Friday nights, a tradition that I've carried from Israel to Harlem.

DORO WOT / DERHO TSEBHI

Spicy Chicken Drumstick Stew

Serves about 8

Doro wot is perhaps the most well-known Ethiopian dish: The mere presence of this rich, fiery chicken stew signifies a rite of passage or a special occasion. Cutting up a whole chicken for doro wot is among the first skills that Ethiopian Jewish mothers teach their daughters. And at meals, each family member is allocated a specific piece of meat based on their status in the household: Honored guests might get the thigh or breast; children the wings. At Ethiopian weddings, the bride and groom are fed by their close friends, a way of showing love, respect, and friendship known as Gursha. While making a truly finger-licking doro wot is a lengthy process, I have carefully streamlined my version over the years to maximize the flavor. See the recipes for Vered's Doro Wot (page 144) and Doro Wot Alicha (page 145) for alternate versions.

2 pounds chicken drumsticks (8–10), skinned

2 tablespoons fresh lemon juice

1 tablespoon fine sea salt

8 large eggs

6 cups Kulet (page 6)

IN A LARGE BOWL, combine the drumsticks, lemon juice, and salt. Add cold water to cover and swish the water around to mix. Soak for at least 10 minutes and up to 1 hour.

Prepare a large bowl of cold water and ice and have nearby. In a medium pot, combine the eggs with cold water to cover. Bring to a boil over medium heat and cook the eggs for 8 minutes. Remove the eggs from the pot and place in the ice bath until completely cooled.

Peel the eggs, leaving them whole. Make four shallow, evenly spaced cuts from top to bottom on each egg, scoring the white but stopping at the yolk.

Meanwhile, in a large pot, heat the kulet over medium heat, stirring occasionally, until simmering.

Drain the water from the drumsticks. Wash the drumsticks well under running water, massaging the chicken and rinsing several times. Submerge in the kulet. Bring back to a simmer and cook gently, stirring occasionally and reducing the heat if the sauce begins to boil, until the drumsticks are completely cooked through, 25 to 30 minutes. During the last 5 minutes of cooking, add the eggs and gently stir to completely submerge them in the sauce. Serve warm.

VERED'S DORO WOT / *DERHO TSEBHI*

Whole Chicken Stew

Serves 6 to 8

There are so many ways to make doro wot: This recipe is adapted from my cousin Vered Gamay's. Her method does not require you to make a separate batch of kulet; instead, she dry-sautés diced onions with garlic and ginger. She also uses a whole chicken, as we commonly did in Ethiopia, and washes it thoroughly with lemons and salt, as is traditional.

CUT THE CHICKEN into 8 to 12 pieces and then remove the skin and fat. In a large bowl, wash the chicken with cold water until the water runs clear. Add the lemon juice, remaining lemon halves, and 1 teaspoon of the salt and add water to cover the chicken. Swish the water around to mix, cover the bowl with plastic wrap, place in the refrigerator, and let the chicken soak for at least 10 minutes and up to 1 hour.

In a large dry pot, add the onions and sauté over medium heat until softened, about 4 minutes. Add the garlic and sauté until fragrant, about 2 minutes. Add the olive oil and ginger, stir well to coat, then add the tomato paste and stir until slightly darkened, about 1 minute. Add the delleh and hot water. Add the korarima, the remaining 1 teaspoon salt, and the pepper.

Drain the chicken. Make two cuts in the largest pieces of chicken and squeeze out the excess juices. Submerge the chicken in the sauce. Cover the pot and simmer, stirring occasionally, until the chicken is cooked through, 40 to 50 minutes.

Taste the stew and add salt if necessary. About 5 minutes before serving, cut a shallow "X" into the top and bottom of each egg and simmer gently over low heat to absorb the flavors. Serve with injera.

1 whole chicken (about 3 pounds), giblets removed

Squeezed juice and halves of 2 lemons (about ¼ cup juice)

2 teaspoons fine sea salt, plus more to taste

4 medium yellow or white onions, diced

10 garlic cloves, minced

½ cup olive oil

2 tablespoons minced fresh ginger

1 (6-ounce) can tomato paste

4 tablespoons Delleh (page 11) or Berbere (page 5)

3 cups hot water

1½ teaspoons Ground Roasted Korarima (page 26)

½ teaspoon black pepper

6-8 hard-boiled eggs (one per person)

Injera (page 37), for serving

DORO WOT ALICHA

Golden Chicken Drumstick Stew

Serves about 5

This is doro wot for those who are sensitive to heat: It leaves out the berbere and relies on small amounts of turmeric, cumin, and korarima to enhance the chicken. People spice it in different ways—for instance, my aunt Genet (Ilana) Mamay (page 219) adds a little bit of delleh and silan (date honey) to hers. I prefer just a single jalapeño pepper, which I leave in larger chunks that will impart their flavor but not add too much heat.

IN A LARGE BOWL, combine the drumsticks, lemon juice, 1 tablespoon of the salt, and cold water to cover. Swish the water around to mix and let the chicken soak for at least 10 minutes and up to 1 hour.

In a food processor, blend the onions until smooth.

Warm a dry Dutch oven or heavy-bottomed medium pot over medium heat. Add the onions, bring to a simmer, and cook, stirring frequently, until most of the water has evaporated and no bubbling liquid can be seen, 30 to 35 minutes.

Add the oil and turmeric and mix constantly until well combined, about 5 minutes.

Drain the water from the drumsticks. Wash the drumsticks well under running water, massaging them and rinsing several times. Add the drumsticks to the pot and cook, stirring frequently and reducing the heat to medium-low if the drumsticks stick to the bottom of the pan, for 10 minutes.

Add 2 cups water and the remaining 2½ teaspoons salt and stir frequently until the chicken is almost cooked through, 5 to 10 minutes. Add the jalapeño, garlic, ginger, cumin, and korarima and simmer, stirring occasionally, until the flavors are integrated and the chicken is cooked through, about 10 minutes.

Taste and add salt if necessary. Garnish with the eggs.

- 2 pounds chicken drumsticks (about 10), skinned
- 2 tablespoons fresh lemon juice
- 1 tablespoon plus 2½ teaspoons fine sea salt, plus more to taste
- 4 yellow onions, quartered
- 1 cup vegetable oil
- ½ teaspoon ground turmeric
- 1 jalapeño, quartered lengthwise
- 2 teaspoons minced garlic
- 1 teaspoon minced fresh ginger
- 1 teaspoon ground cumin
- ¼ teaspoon Ground Roasted Korarima (page 26)
- 5 hard-boiled eggs, halved

SEGA TIBS / *SEGA TIBSI*

Tender Sautéed Beef

Serves 4

This dish honors the tradition of about ten Ethiopian families getting together to split a butchered cow, the fresh meat divided equally according to a process called querecha. No matter where you live, sega tibs makes a classic weeknight meal that comes together quickly, but I encourage you to make this only with the best-quality beef you can find.

IN A LARGE SKILLET, warm 1 tablespoon of the niter kibbeh over medium heat. Add the beef, salt, and pepper and brown the beef on all sides, about 1 minute. Add the onion, jalapeño, ginger, garlic, mitmita, and rosemary and sauté for about 2 minutes.

Pour in the wine, scraping the bottom of the skillet, and sauté until the meat is tender, adding 1 tablespoon water at a time if necessary to keep the mixture saucy, 8 to 10 minutes.

Add the tomato and sauté until softened, about 2 minutes. Drizzle with the remaining 1½ teaspoons niter kibbeh and add salt and pepper to taste. Serve immediately.

1 tablespoon plus 1½ teaspoons Niter Kibbeh (page 15)

1 pound beef tenderloin, cut into bite-sized cubes

½ teaspoon fine sea salt, plus more to taste

½ teaspoon black pepper, plus more to taste

½ red onion, sliced into half-moons

½ jalapeño, cut into thin long strips

¼ teaspoon minced fresh ginger

¼ teaspoon minced garlic

1 teaspoon Mitmita (page 12), or 2 teaspoons Berbere (page 5)

1 sprig fresh rosemary

¼ cup Tej (page 180), white wine, or another sweet wine

½ tomato, cut into bite-sized pieces

DORO TIBS / DERHO TIBSI

Sautéed Chicken with Butter and Herbs

Serves 6 to 8

Here's another weeknight meal that comes together quickly. Marinate boneless, skinless chicken thighs in the morning, then throw this together for dinner later.

IN A LARGE BOWL, whisk together the lemon juice, half of the onion, the garlic, oregano, and basil. Add the chicken thighs and turn to coat. Cover with plastic wrap and marinate for at least 30 minutes at room temperature or up to overnight in the refrigerator.

Remove the chicken and cut into bite-sized cubes. Discard the marinade.

Warm a large skillet over medium heat. Add the chicken, niter kibbeh, thyme sprigs, delleh, salt, and black pepper. Sauté for 1 minute, then add the wine and sauté until reduced, 2 to 3 minutes.

Add the remaining onion, the jalapeño, garlic, and ginger and simmer, stirring occasionally at first, then constantly and rapidly as soon as the dish becomes drier, until the liquid mostly evaporates, red oil bubbles throughout, and the chicken is cooked through and tender, 10 to 12 minutes.

Add the tomato and sauté for about a minute to combine. Serve immediately.

- ½ cup fresh lemon juice
- 1 red onion, minced
- 1 tablespoon minced garlic (about 2 cloves)
- ½ teaspoon dried oregano
- ½ teaspoon dried basil
- 2 pounds boneless, skinless chicken thighs
- 1 tablespoon Niter Kibbeh (page 15)
- 2 sprigs fresh thyme
- 2 tablespoons Delleh (page 11) or Berbere (page 5)
- 1 teaspoon fine sea salt, plus more to taste
- 1 teaspoon black pepper, plus more to taste
- ⅓ cup white wine
- ½ jalapeño, cut into long strips
- ¾ teaspoon minced garlic
- ¼ teaspoon minced fresh ginger
- ½ tomato, cut into bite-sized pieces

ASEFASH MESELE

"They Will Come One Day"

Growing up in a joyful Beta Israel village in Tigray, Asefash Mesele fell asleep at night to the sounds of her grandmother telling her stories of the Old Testament. Asefash knew the names and their stories: Abraham. Sarah. Moses. Each Friday at sundown, she prayed over her family's dabo, made from grains she had milled herself.

Asefash—whose grandfather was the brother of my great-grandmother—also prayed that someday her family would make the journey to Israel, and in the 1960s, she became one of the first to do so. She married Elias, a man from her village who had already studied in Israel in the 1950s, shortly after the founding of the new Jewish state. After he returned to Ethiopia and married Asefash, the two made their way to Asmara, the capital of Eritrea. Eventually, they boarded a ship and sailed through the Red Sea to Southern Israel, arriving in 1968, and becoming one of the first Beta Israel couples to settle in the coastal city of Ashkelon.

Shortly after they arrived, Asefash and her husband traveled to visit one of the holiest sites in all of Judaism, the Cave of Machpelah in Hebron. This is the burial site of many of our most important ancestors—Abraham, Isaac, Jacob, Sarah, Rebecca, and Leah. As she approached the cave, Asefash grew overwhelmed by the memories of her grandmother's nighttime stories. She realized that by visiting this holy place, she was fulfilling her grandmother's deepest wishes—only her grandmother was not there with her. Moved by the experience, she began to weep.

Asefash looked up and saw two women looking at her. "Why is this Black woman crying?" one asked the other. "What is her connection to this?"

Sacrifices for Judaism

Asefash saw that the women did not realize that she—or for that matter, anyone with her skin color—could be Jewish. Asefash was now in the dizzying position of having to prove her Jewishness, even though she knew the Old Testament backward and forward.

This was not the first time she had been doubted. After the birth of their son Asher, she and her husband asked a rabbi to circumcise the child. The rabbi refused, saying he did not think the family was really Jewish. (A friend helped convince another rabbi to do the circumcision.)

Asefash struggled to find her way without the rhythms of Beta Israel life. During her menstrual period, she longed for the special hut that is traditional in Ethiopia. She could not find ingredients to make her family's favorite foods. It would be years before teff or berbere was sold in Israel. It would be even more years before other Beta Israel would be able to settle near her.

Asefash gave birth to her first daughter, Rena, shortly after arriving in Israel. As Rena grew, she realized that she never saw extended family come to visit—no grandparents, aunties, or uncles like her friends had. Rena began asking Asefash why this was.

ASEFASH'S DISHES

Her eyes welling with tears, Asefash promised her daughter, "We do have a very large family. They will come one day."

While they waited, Asefash and her husband found a surrogate family in the community of Jews from Yemen, who had begun immigrating to Israel in 1948. These more established immigrants not only knew what it was like to settle into Israel with dark skin, they also knew how to make food that came close to what Asefash had left behind. Yemenite friends taught her how to make a flatbread called lachuch, which could be made in a single day and was the closest thing to injera that could be found in Israel at the time.

They helped Asefash take care of her children and they supported her endeavors to build a Beta Israel community. Asefach's family eventually managed to establish themselves enough to send money back to Ethiopia and help more and more family members travel to Israel. Her house in Ashkelon became the gathering place for young Ethiopians, who marked the Shabbat every Friday and began to mobilize to make the Beta Israel a force in Israeli politics.

Asefach's story shows the dedication and devotion of people who triumphed over so many doubts and obstacles. Despite not initially feeling welcomed by the Israelis they met, despite having to prove to government officials that they were Jewish, despite decades of sacrifices, and without the food and the family they so deeply cherished, the Beta Israel community held tight to each other and found strength in their devotion to a greater cause.

BERBERE STUFFED PEPPERS with GROUND CHICKEN and BULGUR

Serves 10

My inspiration for this beautiful entrée was Asefash Mesele (page 148), who was born in Tigray and was one of the first Ethiopians to settle in Israel in the 1960s. Asefash loves to stuff peppers with beef and rice. I envisioned making a healthier version of this dish with ground chicken and bulgur, the hearty cracked wheat kernels that are rich in fiber and so popular in Israel. I suggest serving these with Crunchy Sunflower Cabbage Slaw (page 93).

IN A SMALL POT, combine the bulgur with water to cover and a pinch of sea salt. Bring to a boil over medium heat, cover, and cook until tender, 10 to 12 minutes. Drain off any excess water and set aside.

Carefully char the peppers on all sides over an open flame on the stove until lightly blackened, about 3 minutes. (Alternatively, broil them for about 3 minutes, flipping them over halfway.)

Preheat the oven to 350°F. Grease a 9 × 13-inch baking dish.

Place the peppers in the baking dish in a single layer and set aside.

In a dry medium skillet, sauté the onion over medium heat until translucent, about 4 minutes. Add the ginger and garlic, stir, and cook until their raw scent is gone, about 3 minutes. Add the chicken, olive oil, and 2 teaspoons sea salt and sauté, breaking the chicken apart with a wooden spoon, until it is cooked through, 5 to 7 minutes.

Add the tomatoes and cook, breaking them down with a spoon, until the mixture is saucy, about 5 minutes. Add the cooked bulgur, berbere, lime juice, parsley, cilantro, and cumin and stir to combine.

Fill each pepper with ¼ to ⅓ cup of filling, depending on their size. Slide into the oven and bake until the peppers are tender when pierced with a knife, about 20 minutes.

Serve warm.

¾ cup bulgur

Fine sea salt

10 poblano or cubanelle peppers, tops trimmed off and seeded

Vegetable oil, for greasing the pan

1 small red onion, chopped

1 tablespoon minced fresh ginger

3 garlic cloves, minced

8 ounces ground chicken

2 tablespoons olive oil

3 tomatoes, roughly cut into chunks

2 tablespoons Berbere (page 5)

Juice of ½ lime

2 tablespoons chopped fresh parsley

2 tablespoons chopped fresh cilantro

1 teaspoon ground cumin

SCHNITZEL

Aromatic Breaded Fried Chicken

Serves 6 to 8

Schnitzel, traditionally a flattened, fried veal cutlet that originated in Austria, was brought from Europe to Israel by Ashkenazi Jewish immigrants and has since become one of Israel's best-loved dishes. I've put my own spin on it by pounding chicken, combining both Yemenite and Ethiopian seasonings in the breading, and amplifying their flavor with a little chicken bouillon, which many of my relatives use in their cooking.

IN A MEDIUM SHALLOW BOWL, beat the eggs. In a second medium bowl or on a large plate, combine the bread crumbs, sesame seeds, hawaij, berbere, bouillon powder, cumin, turmeric, pepper, and salt (if using).

In a large pan or cast-iron skillet, warm about ½ inch oil over medium heat.

While the oil is heating, arrange an assembly line: Place the bowl of bread crumbs closest to the stove and the bowl of eggs next to it. Place the chicken on a platter next to the eggs. Line a plate with paper towels and place it nearby.

Test the heat of the oil by sprinkling a pinch of the bread crumbs into the pan; the oil is hot enough when small white bubbles foam and rise to the surface.

Using one hand, dunk the first piece of chicken in the eggs and shake off the excess. Coat both sides in bread crumbs. Add to the oil and fry until golden brown on both sides, 3 to 4 minutes per side. Drain on the paper towels. Working in batches, continue with the rest of the chicken, reducing the heat if the chicken is browning too quickly.

2 large eggs

1 cup dried bread crumbs

2 tablespoons white sesame seeds

1 tablespoon Hawaij (page 22)

1 tablespoon Berbere (page 5)

1 teaspoon chicken bouillon powder

1 teaspoon ground cumin

½ teaspoon ground turmeric

½ teaspoon black pepper

½ teaspoon fine sea salt (omit if bread crumbs contain salt)

Vegetable oil, for frying

3 pounds boneless, skinless chicken breasts, sliced or pounded as thinly as possible

KAI WOT / ZIGNI

Traditional Spicy, Hearty Beef Stew

Serves 8

Blazing with flavor and color, kai wot—Amharic for "red stew"—is a must at many special occasions and a beautiful addition to the Shabbat table. This is my favorite way to make it, using beef chuck and a healthy amount of berbere.

IN A DRY SAUCEPAN, simmer the onions over medium heat until most of the water has evaporated, about 10 minutes.

Add the oil, berbere, garlic, and ginger. Reduce the heat to medium-low and simmer, stirring occasionally, for 5 minutes to combine the flavors.

In a large bowl, mix the chuck with the lemon juice and rinse with cold water, pouring off the blood and impurities. Add the beef and salt to the pan, cover, and simmer, stirring frequently, until the beef is cooked through, about 15 minutes.

Add the warm water and korarima and continue to simmer until the meat collapses and becomes meltingly tender, another 45 minutes to 1 hour, adding more warm water when necessary, ½ cup at a time, to keep the sauce loose and bubbling and the meat moist.

Taste and add salt if necessary. If desired, drizzle with niter kibbeh and serve warm.

4 large or 5 medium red onions, cut into chunks and blended in a food processor

1 cup vegetable oil

⅔ cup Berbere (page 5)

2 teaspoons minced garlic

1 teaspoon minced fresh ginger

2 pounds beef chuck, cut into ¼-inch cubes

Juice of ½ lemon

1 teaspoon fine sea salt, plus more to taste

1 cup warm water, plus more as needed

½ teaspoon Ground Roasted Korarima (page 26)

¼ cup Niter Kibbeh (page 15; optional), melted

RISHAN'S KAI WOT / *SEGA TSEBHI*

Israeli-Influenced Spicy, Hearty Beef Stew

Serves 6 to 8

My aunt Rishan Mesele (page 44) learned to cook as a child in Ethiopia and initially struggled to adapt to what was available in Israel. Now, though, her version of the spicy red kai wot beef stew reflects decades of Israeli influence. She cooks and spices it differently than I do: She uses chopped onions for a slightly chunkier version, and the bouillon powder adds a saltier chicken flavor.

IN A MEDIUM POT, warm the oil over medium heat. Add the onion and garlic and sauté until browned, about 15 minutes.

Add the tomato paste and mix constantly for 3 to 4 minutes. Add the berbere and stir well for 1 minute. Stir in the hot water and bouillon powder and simmer until thickened, 10 to 15 minutes.

Add the beef, salt, and black pepper, reduce the heat to low, and simmer for 30 minutes. Add the cumin, korarima, and cayenne (if using) and simmer until the meat is tender, 30 minutes to 1 hour, adding more hot water when necessary, ½ cup at a time, to keep the sauce loose and bubbling. Taste and adjust the salt.

Serve over injera or with rice.

½ cup vegetable oil

1 red onion, chopped

6 garlic cloves, minced

2 tablespoons tomato paste

2 tablespoons Berbere (page 5)

1 cup hot water, plus more as needed

1 tablespoon chicken bouillon powder

2 pounds beef chuck, cut into ½-inch cubes

1 teaspoon fine sea salt, plus more to taste

½ teaspoon black pepper

½ teaspoon ground cumin

½ teaspoon Ground Roasted Korarima (page 26)

½ teaspoon cayenne pepper (optional, for a spicier stew)

Injera (page 37) or cooked rice, for serving

KITFO

Beef Canapés

Makes about 10 canapés

These pretty canapés may not follow the Beta Israel tradition of keeping dairy and meat separate, but they are cherished by non-Jewish Ethiopians. The secret to making exceptional Ethiopian kitfo beef tartare is starting with *hot* niter kibbeh and mixing the beef quickly. My tip: Do all of the preparation in advance. This will allow you to assemble the canapés right before serving, and ensure that the beef cooks just enough.

CUT THE INJERA into 10 small rounds 2 inches across. Toast them on both sides in a dry pan until crisp but pliable, about 2 minutes.

Finely chop the beef as finely as possible in a food processor or meat grinder, or by hand.

In a medium pot, warm the niter kibbeh over medium heat. Reduce the heat to the barest minimum and add the beef tenderloin, mitmita, korarima, salt, and pepper. Stir vigorously to combine.

Immediately spoon onto the injera rounds. If desired, garnish with the gomen and ayib.

1 (10-inch) Injera (page 37) or 10 large Injera Chips (page 43) or, in a pinch, pita chips

1 pound beef tenderloin, preferably grass-fed

½ cup Niter Kibbeh (page 15), butter, or ghee

1 teaspoon Mitmita (page 12)

½ teaspoon Ground Roasted Korarima (page 26)

¼ teaspoon fine sea salt

⅛ teaspoon black pepper

Gomen (page 107; optional), for garnish

Ayib (page 18) or feta cheese (optional), for garnish

BEG WOT / *BEGI TSEBHI*

Holiday Lamb Stew

Serves 8

Lamb is a staple on the holiday tables of so many Jewish families. We Beta Israel serve this aromatic dish to commemorate the Torah-mandated sacrifice of the paschal lamb on Passover, and to celebrate the beginning of a new year on Rosh Hashanah. Cooking the lamb until it is falling apart is absolutely crucial to the success of this stew. If in doubt, cook longer! You can also substitute goat (fiyel in Amharic), as we often did in Ethiopia; the cooking times may change.

3 pounds bone-in lamb loin chops

Juice of ½ lemon

2 cups Kulet (page 6)

2 teaspoons minced garlic

1 teaspoon minced fresh ginger

1 teaspoon fine sea salt

½ teaspoon Ground Roasted Korarima (page 26)

¼ cup Niter Kibbeh (page 15; optional)

PUT THE LAMB CHOPS in a large bowl and add the lemon juice and cold water to cover. Swish the meat back and forth for several minutes, then soak for about 10 minutes.

Slice the majority of the lamb meat off the chops and cut into 1-inch pieces.

In a large dry pot, combine the lamb meat, the meaty bones, and kulet. Stir frequently over medium heat until the meat is lightly browned and the kulet begins to caramelize on the bottom of the pot, 10 to 15 minutes.

Add the garlic and ginger and cook, stirring frequently, until fragrant, 2 to 3 minutes. Add 2 cups water and the salt. Scrape any mixture stuck to the bottom of the pot, reduce the heat to medium-low, and cook until the meat is soft, tender, and falling apart, 30 to 40 minutes.

Add the korarima and niter kibbeh (if using). Cook for 5 to 10 minutes to integrate the flavors. Serve warm, with the bones (guests can feel free to gnaw off excess meat).

YEMENITE CHICKEN SOUP

Serves 8

I adapted this deeply flavored chicken soup from the recipe of my dear friend Dr. Ephraim Isaac (page 238), a prominent half-Ethiopian, half-Yemenite academic and leader. I would love for it to be one of the first dishes that Americans think of when they think of "Jewish foods," right alongside Ashkenazi favorites.

Dr. Isaac married a fellow academic who is Ashkenazi, and they raised two daughters and a son in Princeton, New Jersey. Each Shabbat while raising their family, they enjoyed this chicken soup, as well as foods like hummus and zhoug that were still years away from hitting the mainstream.

Dr. Isaac's elder daughter, Devorah, remembers regarding the foods of her childhood as oddities, a cuisine that set her apart from her classmates. Now as an adult, she proudly teaches her own children the Ethiopian and Yemenite traditions she grew up with. She also shared with me a twist that you can feel free to try: Her children love dunking the Ashkenazi matzah balls in their Yemenite soup. "It is a match made in heaven," she said.

MAKE THE CHICKEN SOUP: In a large bowl, massage the chicken with the lemon juice and 1 tablespoon of the salt. Let sit at room temperature for at least 5 minutes and up to 30 minutes. Rinse the chicken well.

Place the chicken in a large stockpot and add cold water to cover by 1 to 2 inches. Cover the pot and bring to a boil over high heat. Uncover and boil, periodically skimming off any foam that rises to the top, for about 30 minutes.

Add the onions, carrots, celery, garlic, parsley, ¼ cup of the cilantro, the hawaij, the remaining 1 tablespoon salt, and the pepper. Reduce the heat to medium and simmer uncovered until the soup is a deep yellow, 30 to 45 minutes.

Taste and adjust the seasoning, if necessary. If the flavor is too concentrated, add a little water.

Divide among eight bowls, placing a whole small onion (or half a large onion) in each bowl. Serve with the lemon wedges, hilbe, and zhoug.

CHICKEN SOUP

- 1 whole chicken (4–5 pounds), cut into 8–12 pieces (including backbone), or 4–5 pounds drumsticks
- ¼ cup fresh lemon juice
- 2 tablespoons fine sea salt, plus more to taste
- 8 small red or white onions, peeled and left whole, or use 4 large onions, halved
- 4 large carrots, peeled and cut into ½-inch rounds
- 1 cup chopped celery
- 10 garlic cloves, chopped
- ½ cup chopped fresh parsley
- ¼ cup plus 2 tablespoons chopped fresh cilantro leaves and stems
- 3 tablespoons Hawaij (page 22)
- 1 tablespoon black pepper, plus more to taste

FOR SERVING

Lemon wedges

Hilbe (page 21)

Zhoug (page 25)

ASSA WOT / ASSA TSEBHI

Shabbat Fish Stew

Serves 4 to 6

I associate this fish stew with marking the Shabbat during my early childhood in Ethiopia. My grandmother would walk to the market, buy the freshest fish, and make assa wot ahead of time to savor during the quiet, sacred hours between sundown Friday and sundown Saturday. She also made it when someone caught something particularly impressive. I like this with salmon, but feel free to use any kind of meaty fish that holds up to the thick stew: halibut, sea bass, even branzino.

1½ pounds skinless salmon fillets (see Note), cut into 1-inch cubes

¾ teaspoon fine sea salt

¼ teaspoon black pepper

2 tablespoons Niter Kibbeh (page 15)

2¼ cups Kulet (page 6), warm or at room temperature

SEASON THE FISH with the salt and pepper.

In a medium cast-iron skillet, warm the niter kibbeh over medium-low heat. Add the fish cubes in a single layer and sauté on all sides until lightly browned, 2 to 3 minutes.

Add the kulet, making sure that it covers all of the fish. Reduce the heat to low and simmer while gently stirring, taking care not to break up the chunks, until the fish is cooked through, 2 to 3 minutes. Serve warm.

Note You can substitute your favorite fish, but you may need to adjust the cooking time.

SPICY TOMATO TILAPIA

Serves 6

My aunt Rishan Mesele (page 44) loves to make this zesty fish dish on the Sabbath. In Israel, it's common to have a fish dish on Friday night, and I love how this is similar to the African American tradition of frying fish on Fridays. Tilapia is popular in Israel, and Rishan combines it with Ethiopian flavors to give it a taste of our birthplace. Feel free to use any mild white fish.

IN A MEDIUM SAUCEPAN, cook the tomatoes over medium-low heat until they are soft and begin to break down, 8 to 10 minutes.

Add the olive oil and onion and cook until translucent, about 4 minutes. Add the serrano and garlic and simmer until softened, 5 to 7 minutes. Mix in the cilantro, parsley, tomato paste, salt, black pepper, cumin, bouillon powder, paprika, berbere, and cayenne (if using). Add 1 cup water, mix, and simmer until thickened, about 15 minutes.

Taste and adjust the salt, if necessary. Add the tilapia, coating with the sauce, and simmer without moving the fish until cooked through, about 30 minutes.

Serve garnished with cilantro.

6 plum tomatoes, chopped

½ cup olive oil

1 medium red onion, thinly sliced

1 serrano pepper, minced

8 garlic cloves, sliced

2 tablespoons chopped fresh cilantro leaves and stems, plus more for garnish

2 tablespoons chopped fresh parsley

3 tablespoons tomato paste

1 teaspoon fine sea salt, plus more to taste

½ teaspoon black pepper

½ teaspoon ground cumin

1 tablespoon chicken bouillon powder

1 tablespoon sweet paprika

1 tablespoon Berbere (page 5)

½ teaspoon cayenne pepper (optional; for a spicier stew)

6 skinless tilapia fillets (6 ounces each) or another mild white fish

BERBERE FRIED FISH

Serves 8

Another fish dish for Fridays (or any day you wish), this one combines the flavors of my childhood home of Ethiopia with the fried fish that's so popular in my adult home of Harlem. Historians say the tradition of African American fish fries originated because enslaved people were given Saturday to themselves, and they often fished and fried their own dinners. The tradition eventually moved to Fridays (perhaps because of the influence of Catholics, who often eat fish on Fridays during Lent). It exists all week long in my Harlem neighborhood, home to some of the country's best fried fish spots. This fish makes an outstanding taco (see Injera Fish Tacos, page 167).

Juice of 1 lemon

8 tilapia fillets (6 ounces each)

½ cup all-purpose flour

¼ cup Berbere (page 5)

1 teaspoon ground cumin

½ teaspoon fine sea salt, plus more to taste

½ teaspoon black pepper

2 large eggs

Vegetable oil, for frying

IN A BOWL, combine the lemon juice and water. Add the fish fillets and gently swish around. Soak for 10 minutes, then drain.

On a shallow plate, whisk together the flour, berbere, cumin, salt, and pepper. In a wide, shallow bowl, beat the eggs. Set a wire rack in a sheet pan or line a large plate with paper towels.

Pour 1 inch of oil into a large cast-iron skillet or Dutch oven and heat over medium heat until 280°F on a deep-fry thermometer.

Pick up one piece of fish and dip it in the eggs to coat both sides, shaking off any excess. Then dip in the seasoned flour, coating both sides and shaking off the excess. Place the fish in the oil and fry until the fish is cooked through and golden brown, flipping halfway, 2 to 3 minutes on each side, depending on the thickness of the fish. Drain on the rack or paper towels.

INJERA FISH TACOS

Serves 4

Save some Berbere Fried Fish to make this pretty Ethiopian spin on a fish taco.

PLACE THE ROUNDS OF INJERA on a plate. Top each with a piece of fish, some cabbage slaw, and awaze to taste. Serve with lime wedges.

1 (10-inch) Injera (page 37), cut into 4 equal rounds

2 fillets Berbere Fried Fish (page 163), each cut in half

About ½ cup Crunchy Sunflower Cabbage Slaw (page 93) or shredded red cabbage

Awaze (page 32)

4 lime wedges

CHAPTER 7

DRINKS AND PASTRY

It's impossible to overstate the importance of coffee, tea, honey wine, and other drinks to Beta Israel culture: Each is rooted in ritual and used to mark everything from ordinary mornings to important milestones. This chapter details the most important ones.

Pastry, on the other hand, came later in my journey. Dessert is not traditionally part of Ethiopian cuisine. The first time I remember seeing dough fried was in Sudan, and I discovered a love for sweet desserts in Israel. My pastry recipes incorporate influences from baked goods popular in both Israel and the United States.

BUNA / BUNN

Coffee for Prosperity

Serves 8 to 10

We Ethiopian families regard coffee—roasting it, serving it, drinking it—as a major part of daily life, not something to grab on the run. I remember waking up to the crackling of a fire, the smell of smoke, the sound of rattling coffee beans, and eventually the aroma of freshly roasting coffee. This roasting ritual was seen as a way to cleanse the air and start the day anew. It often signifies a time to come together, to discuss the day's issues or just gossip, and it can last for hours. After roasting the beans, it's customary to present the hot pan to your guests, who will wave their hands over it three times and issue a blessing to the lady of the house, saying, "May thy home be prosperous."

Traditionally, Ethiopian coffee is served from a special pot called a jebena, and poured from high up, so that the coffee splatters like a babbling brook. It's served in small, strong servings in espresso-like cups known as sini. Often, the same coffee grounds will be used to make three rounds, all of which are delicious but vary in their strength. The first is called abol (awel in Tigrinya), and has the thickest consistency. The second round, tona (kalai), is more diluted, and the third round, baraka (berekah), is the most diluted, and often given to children to sample. None of these is served with milk or sugar, though many coffee-drinkers enjoy adding a bit of Niter Kibbeh (page 15).

Coffee is so important that roasting it for someone else is considered an honor. Vered Germay (page 8), my cousin, was so close to my mother that she was one of the last people to roast coffee for her before she died. It is said that by the last cup, a transformation of the spirit takes place.

½ cup green (unroasted) coffee beans (available online or at some specialty coffee shops)

5 green cardamom pods (optional)

5 whole cloves (optional)

Niter Kibbeh (page 15; optional), about 1 teaspoon per serving

Pinch of fine sea salt (optional)

IN A MEDIUM NONSTICK PAN, combine the beans and ¼ cup water. Wash the beans two or three times, pouring out and adding ¼ cup water each time, rubbing the beans with your fingers until the translucent skins come off.

Pour out the standing water and place the pan over medium heat. Add the cardamom and cloves (if using). Stir and swirl the beans constantly to roast evenly. They will go from green to yellow

Buna / Bunn continues

to brown, taking on a shine as they release their oils. Remove them from the heat when they are deep brown and shiny, 10 to 12 minutes.

Use a coffee grinder to grind the beans (and spices, if using) to a medium grind. Pour the grinds into a small pot. Add 2 cups water and bring to a boil over medium heat. Boil for 10 to 12 minutes. Strain through cheesecloth or a coffee filter.

To serve, pour ¼ cup into each espresso cup. If desired, add niter kibbeh and/or salt to taste.

MEHRATA (MALKA) LEMLEM AVRAHAM

Peace and Prosperity

Three weeks into my village's journey out of Ethiopia, my mother's close friend Mehrata Lemlem Avraham began feeling labor pains. We had set off while Mehrata was heavily pregnant with her first child, and the other women in the village had huddled around her through the long nights of travel, making sure she ate, drank, and rested.

The entire group had stopped to rest and eat somewhere near the Ethiopia-Sudan border, and that's when Mehrata's baby girl arrived, eased out by the willing hands of the other women. Mehrata gave her daughter the name Gaula, which means "redemption."

The weeks after an Ethiopian Jewish woman gives birth are considered sacred. The new mother is isolated in a special house, known as the Harrase Gojo ("The House of the New Mother"), where she can bond with her baby, and be supported by other women who will cook for her, wash her clothes, and do other chores. Since her baby was a girl, Mehrata would ordinarily have been confined to this house for eighty days (forty for a boy).

Mehrata had lived her entire life expecting to do this when she gave birth. But at this perilous time, it was impossible. Our group had left the only home we had ever known and were midjourney, in the middle of the desert. At the time, we had stopped near a side road that was being patrolled by Ethiopian authorities. We risked being captured if we lingered too long, and of course, no one would leave Mehrata and her baby behind.

So just fifteen minutes after giving birth, Mehrata climbed back on a horse. The other women dug into sacks of flaxseed and mixed it with water, so that Mehrata could sip a steady supply of the drink known as Telva (page 177), which would help keep her strong. Her baby daughter was given to a cousin to nurse. And the group kept going.

Mehrata was firm in her belief that all these sacrifices would be worth it when we reached the Holy Land. She felt some relief upon reaching Sudan, where we lived for two years before traveling to Israel: "It was a joyous moment," she remembers. When we arrived in Israel, she was given the Hebrew name of Malka—which means "queen." While this name happened to suit her perfectly, she prefers to go by the Ethiopian name she was given at birth.

In addition to adjusting to a new name, she was also adjusting to new ways of cooking. Ever since she was young, Mehrata had roasted her own coffee from her family's beans, and her family made berbere from their own peppers, injera from teff or sorghum, beer from sorghum and barley, and cheese, yogurt, and butter from fresh cow's milk.

But once we reached the Holy Land, years went by before Mehrata, my mother, and the other families could find teff flour. So Mehrata learned to make injera in a nonstick pan, using white and wheat flours. She dried peppers, onions, and garlic, and

MEHRATA'S DISH

177 Telva

found a mill that would grind them into her own berbere blend. For the first time, she used frozen chicken to make doro wot. She had grown up serving the chicken parts according to family status but found that tradition was not observed in Israel.

The challenge of feeding their families with unfamiliar ingredients drew the women in the Beta Israel community close together. Mehrata and my mother had known each other only casually in Ethiopia, but they became close friends in Israel. Eventually, they became part of a sixteen-woman social group that rotated among each other's houses, eating lentil stew and collard greens, roasting coffee, exchanging ideas and emotional support, and providing financial support to each other when needed by pooling their money (known as an Equb).

Mehrata's daughter Gaula is now grown. The family eventually settled in Kiryat Malakhi, a city in Southern Israel, which is home to a large population of Ethiopian Jews. While Mehrata still cooks Ethiopian food, she struggles to get her children to follow suit.

When I cook these recipes, lucky enough to have access to the right ingredients, I think of my mother and Mehrata finding their way in a new country, making do with what they had. And when I celebrate the Shabbat, I think of Mehrata continuing to observe Beta Israel traditions even in the hardest of times. "From respecting and observing the Shabbat, only good things can come upon us," she told me. And when she does so each week, she says, "I hope for peace and prosperity."

TELVA / ENTATI

Flaxseed Drink

Serves 6 to 8

I like to sip this filling, fiber-packed drink in the morning, and around Passover. It has such a humble appearance, and you would never know at first glance that it is actually one of the great superheroes of the Beta Israel journey out of Ethiopia. This was particularly true for my mother's close friend Mehrata Lemlem Avraham (profiled on page 174), who gave birth while we were en route to Sudan.

½ cup brown or golden flaxseeds

4 cups unsweetened almond milk or whole milk (for a thicker consistency)

About ¼ cup honey, agave, or maple syrup, or to taste (optional)

1 banana (optional)

WARM A LARGE NONSTICK PAN over medium heat. Pour in the flaxseeds and stir so they are in a single layer. Roast, stirring occasionally. The seeds will begin to crackle and pop. Remove from the heat when the popping grows loud, after about 4 minutes. Transfer to a plate or shallow bowl to cool completely.

Transfer the seeds to a clean coffee grinder and grind finely. Stop grinding while the flaxseed is still loose and dry; if you grind it too long, it will turn moist and clumpy.

Add the ground flaxseed to a blender. Add the almond milk and blend until smooth. If using the honey and banana, add them and blend until incorporated. Refrigerate before drinking. (Do not heat this blended mixture; it will be too clumpy to drink.)

Note If you want to serve the telva hot: Omit the almond milk and the banana. Add 2 tablespoons ground toasted flaxseeds to 1 cup boiling water for each serving. Add honey to taste.

SHAHI / *SHAI*   Ethiopian Spiced Tea

Serves 6

I make this refreshing beverage with lots of aromatics. It will give
you a concentrate that you can dilute to your liking by adding hot
water. While I love to sip the spiced mixture on its own, you can easily add a black tea bag, too.

3″ piece fresh ginger, peeled and
  roughly sliced

6 cinnamon sticks

1 tablespoon green cardamom
  pods

1 tablespoon whole cloves

  Black tea bags (optional),
  1 per serving

IN A MEDIUM POT, combine the ginger, cinnamon sticks, cardamom,
cloves, and 4 cups cold water and bring to a boil over high heat.
Boil until the liquid is deep brown and fragrant, 15 to 20 minutes.

Strain the liquid and discard the solids. This is the concentrate.

Dilute with hot water: I like to add 2 parts water to 1 part tea
concentrate. At this point, if using a tea bag, you can bring the
diluted drink to a boil and steep to your desired strength.

TEJ / *MES*   Royal Honey Wine

Makes about 4 quarts

Ethiopia has long been a major producer of honey, and this fermented wine, often made at home, is the sweet, fizzy result. For centuries, African buckhorn leaves, called gesho, have been used to make tej: Ethiopian kings and queens sipped tej out of bereles, elegant round drinking flasks. Nowadays, both gesho leaves and bereles are available online, and you can easily make your own honey wine using this recipe I adapted from my aunt Genet (Ilana) Mamay's.

½ cup gesho leaves

1 unpeeled fresh turmeric root, cut lengthwise into 4 pieces

3½ cups honey

IN A MEDIUM POT, bring the gesho and 3 cups water to a boil over medium heat. Turn off the heat and let sit while you prepare the rest of the ingredients.

In a 5-quart glass or plastic container, combine the turmeric and 8 cups water. Stir in the honey.

Add the gesho water to the container. Cover and let sit at room temperature for at least 1 week and up to 1 month, popping the lid every few days to release any gas, until the honey ferments and smells alcoholic.

Strain and store in the refrigerator for up to 2 months.

SUFF DRINK

Sunflower Seed Drink

Serves 1

My beloved sunflower seeds make an excellent hearty tonic, especially for those times when you are avoiding meat and dairy. The sugar mitigates the bitterness, but feel free to leave it out if you prefer.

1 cup Suff Base (page 28)
1 teaspoon sugar (optional)

IN A GLASS, mix the suff base and the sugar (if using).

SPRIS   Tricolored Layered Smoothie

Makes about 6 cups (serves 3 or 4)

The first time I was able to return to Ethiopia as an adult, I became entranced by the juice stands on the street in the capital of Addis Ababa. The tricolored layered smoothies, known as spris, became my favorite quick, refreshing snack, and now I love making them at home. Here I use avocado, mango, and papaya to represent the three colors of the Ethiopian flag, but feel free to swap them out for pineapple, guava, strawberries . . . the possibilities are endless. This also makes a beautiful smoothie bowl, perhaps topped with the other half of the papaya, toasted pecans, and chopped dates.

½ papaya, peeled, seeded, and cut into chunks (about 1½ pounds fruit)

1 large mango (about 1 pound), peeled, pitted, and cut into chunks

1 large or 2 small avocados (about 1 pound), halved and pitted

3–4 lime wedges or slices, for garnish

IN A BLENDER, preferably high-powered, pour in ½ cup cold water, then add the papaya chunks. Blend until smooth. Divide evenly among serving glasses.

Rinse out the blender and add ¼ cup water. Add the mango chunks and blend until smooth. Pour on top of the papaya in the serving glasses, dividing evenly.

Rinse out the blender and add ¼ cup water. Scoop in the avocado flesh, adding more water, a tablespoon at a time, if necessary to blend, until smooth. Pour on top of the mango in the serving glasses, dividing evenly.

Add a lime wedge or slice to each glass. Serve immediately, with a long spoon or straw.

SORREL (HIBISCUS) CONCENTRATE

*Makes 2 quarts
(serves about 16 when diluted)*

My husband grew up on the Caribbean island of Dominica, and I have loved learning about his native food. One of my favorites is agua de Jamaica, an iced tea made from sorrel (hibiscus) and infused with ginger. I later discovered that similar drinks can be found in many West African cultures, too: called bissap in Senegal, and zobo in Nigeria. This is my version, which adds a fruity kick from pineapple and oranges, with hints of cinnamon and cloves. This recipe makes an unsweetened concentrate. Simply mix 1 part concentrate to 2 parts water, and add sweetener to your liking. Try experimenting with sparkling water, or use the concentrate as the base for a cocktail.

About 1 cup (2¼ ounces) dried sorrel (also known as hibiscus flowers)

½ cup roughly chopped pineapple, fresh or frozen

2 small oranges, cut into wedges

1 small apple, cut into wedges

1 ounce fresh ginger, roughly chopped (feel free to double for a spicier drink)

1 cinnamon stick

¼ teaspoon whole cloves

Simple syrup, honey, or maple syrup (optional)

Ice

IN A LARGE POT, combine the sorrel, pineapple, oranges, apple, ginger, cinnamon stick, cloves, and 2½ quarts water and bring to a boil over high heat. Reduce the heat to medium and boil vigorously for 30 minutes.

Remove from the heat and let sit until the mixture comes to room temperature (overnight is fine, if necessary).

Pour through a strainer to remove the solids. Store the concentrate in the refrigerator.

For a single serving, combine ½ cup concentrate with 1 cup water. Add sweetener to taste, pour over ice, and serve.

REDD FOXX COCKTAIL

Makes 1 cocktail

In the 1930s and '40s, the space that now houses Tsion Café was home to Jimmy's Chicken Shack, a Harlem institution where Malcolm X waited tables and the comedian Redd Foxx washed dishes. I thought Mr. Foxx deserved his own cocktail, with a bright hue as vibrant as he was. Note that simple syrup can be purchased, but it is also easy to make: simply melt 1 cup sugar into 1 cup water and cool.

3 ounces Sorrel (Hibiscus) Concentrate (page 187)
1 ounce fresh lime juice
3 ounces tequila or vodka
½ ounce simple syrup
  Slice of jalapeño
1 ounce ginger beer

FILL A COCKTAIL SHAKER WITH ICE, then pour in the sorrel concentrate, lime juice, tequila, and simple syrup. Add the jalapeño slice, shake to combine, and strain into a glass. Pour the ginger beer on top.

KAFFA MARTINI

Makes 1 cocktail

This popular Tsion Café cocktail is named for the Kaffa region in Ethiopia, the birthplace of coffee, and is a festive nod to the importance of coffee to Ethiopians. We make it with Amarula, a cream liqueur from South Africa.

1 ounce Ethiopian Coffee Extract (page 33)

1 ounce Amarula or Bailey's

¼ ounce simple syrup

1 shot of espresso (optional)

A few coffee beans, for garnish

FILL A COCKTAIL SHAKER WITH ICE. Add the coffee extract, Amarula, simple syrup, and espresso (if using). Shake well. Strain and pour into a chilled martini glass. Garnish with a few coffee beans.

MALAWACH Flaky Flatbread

Makes 10 flatbreads

In Israel, malawach is popular morning fare among the Yemenite Jewish community, served with hard-boiled eggs, tomatoes, and zhoug. At Tsion Café, we sprinkle malawach with coconut and honey and serve it for dessert: It's one of our most-ordered menu items. If you'd like to keep some in the freezer, fully shape the malawach into snail shapes, then place parchment paper between them, transfer to a freezer bag or airtight container, and store in the freezer. Thaw in the refrigerator before frying.

IN A STAND MIXER fitted with the dough hook, combine the lukewarm water, butter, and champagne vinegar. Sprinkle the flour, salt, sugar, and baking powder on top and mix on medium, stopping the machine periodically to scrape down the sides and adding more water, a tablespoon at a time, if necessary, until the dough is smooth, soft, and elastic, 7 to 8 minutes. Place in a bowl, cover with plastic wrap, and let rest at room temperature for 30 minutes.

Line a sheet pan with parchment paper. Turn the dough out onto a non-floured surface and use a sharp knife or a bench scraper to divide it into 10 equal pieces, weighing about 90 grams each. Take one dough ball and roll it into a rough circle, 10 to 12 inches in diameter. The dough should be thin and slightly translucent. Repeat with the remaining balls.

Using a pastry brush, brush the entire surface of the dough with niter kibbeh. Starting from the edge closest to you, use your hands to roll the dough away from you into a tight, long log resembling a jelly roll. Next, shape the log into a snail shape, tucking the tail end under it, and place on the lined sheet pan. Continue until all the dough balls are shaped into snails, placing them 1 inch apart. Cover with plastic wrap and refrigerate for at least 30 minutes to firm up.

Preheat the oven to 195°F. On a dry surface, roll each snail out into a 9-inch circle, placing parchment paper on top of each fully shaped circle, if stacking them, to prevent them from sticking together.

In a medium nonstick skillet, warm 1 teaspoon niter kibbeh and

1 cup lukewarm water, plus more if necessary

5 tablespoons (70 grams) unsalted butter, at room temperature

2 teaspoons champagne vinegar

4 cups (520 grams) all-purpose flour

1 tablespoon plus 1½ teaspoons (23 grams) fine sea salt

2 tablespoons (25 grams) sugar

2 teaspoons baking powder

½ cup (113 grams) Niter Kibbeh (page 15), melted and slightly cooled, plus more for frying

Vegetable oil, for frying

Berbere (page 5; optional)

For serving, as a dessert: honey and shredded coconut (optional)

For serving, as breakfast: hard-boiled eggs, chopped tomatoes, and Zhoug (page 25)

1 teaspoon oil over medium-low heat. Cook the malawach until crisp and lightly browned on both sides, about 3 minutes on each side. Transfer to a sheet pan and store in the oven while frying the remaining malawach. Add niter kibbeh and oil after frying each malawach to attain the desired crispiness.

To serve as a dessert: Drizzle with honey and sprinkle with coconut.

To serve as breakfast: Pair with hard-boiled eggs, chopped tomatoes, and zhoug.

LEGAMAT

Fresh Sudanese Doughnuts

Makes 12 small doughnuts

The smell of frying dough always takes me back to the years of my childhood that I spent in Sudan, waiting to enter Israel. Our Sudanese neighbors were so welcoming to me, and so were vendors on the street, who handed me free oranges and invited me to try the little doughnuts they were frying.

Though dessert is not part of ancient Ethiopian food culture, many of my family began making it in Israel. My aunt Shiwaynish Tzgai (page 121) has embraced the tradition of doughnuts around Hanukkah, and to honor her and the generous Sudanese street vendors of my youth, I created these celebratory doughnuts, laced with the flavors of Shahi (page 206).

1⅓ cups (320 grams) warm water

½ teaspoon active dry yeast

¼ cup (50 grams) sugar

2 cups (280 grams) all-purpose flour

1 teaspoon baking powder

½ teaspoon salt

1 teaspoon Shahi Spice Mix (from Shahi-Spiced Praline Babka, page 206), or a pinch of nutmeg plus ⅛ teaspoon ground cinnamon

Neutral oil, for shallow-frying

2 tablespoons powdered sugar

IN A MEDIUM BOWL, whisk together the warm water, yeast, and sugar. Let the mixture stand and get bubbly for 5 minutes.

In a separate bowl, sift together the flour, baking powder, salt, and spices. Add the dry ingredients to the wet and use a spatula to combine. Cover the dough with a clean towel or plastic wrap and let sit in a warm place for 30 minutes.

Line a plate with a paper towel or clean towel and have nearby. Pour ½ inch of oil into a 9-inch cast-iron skillet or wide shallow pot and warm over medium-high heat until shimmering.

Working in batches of 5 at a time, use two spoons or an ice cream scoop to carefully drop about 2 tablespoons of batter into the hot oil. Fry until golden brown all over, 3 to 4 minutes on each side. Drain the doughnuts on the towel.

Sprinkle with powdered sugar before serving.

Storage Store in an airtight container for up to 3 days.

HIMBASHA / AMBASHA

Ashenda Cake with Honey and Cinnamon

Serves 6 to 8

With its slight sweetness and unique pattern and designs that each baker customizes, himbasha mark special holidays and are a treat that children look forward to eating. My aunt Terfinish Ferede associates this cake with Ashenda, the holiday that celebrates women and girls: She remembers dressing up, dancing and singing with her friends, then being offered slices of this cake, drizzled with a little honey.

IN A STAND MIXER fitted with the dough hook, add the warm water and sprinkle the yeast and sugar on top. Let stand for 5 minutes.

Whisk in the honey and oil. Add the all-purpose flour, einkorn flour, salt, cinnamon, and cardamom and mix on low speed, scraping down the bowl periodically, for 4 minutes. Add the raisins and mix on medium-low until the dough is stretchy and elastic, about 3 minutes. Shape the dough into a ball, place in a bowl, cover with plastic wrap, and let rise at room temperature until doubled in size, 1 hour to 1½ hours.

Grease a 10-inch round cake pan or line a sheet pan with parchment. Lightly flour the surface of the dough, flip it onto a clean counter, and shape into a 10-inch round. If you are using a cake pan, carefully move the dough into the pan, flattening the surface. If you are using a sheet pan, move the dough to the pan and create a flat top on your dough using the palms of your hands.

Using a sharp knife, cut a cross from top to bottom and left to right. Continue to cut concentric lines about one-third of the way through the dough in a pattern of your choice. You can also use a fork to create your own motif. Once designed to your liking, cover with a clean towel or plastic wrap and proof at room temperature until the dough has risen and is puffy, 30 minutes to 1 hour.

Preheat the oven to 350°F.

Remove the plastic wrap and brush the top of the himbasha with the milk. Bake until golden brown, 30 to 40 minutes.

Let cool in the cake pan or on the sheet pan until cool enough to handle and then transfer to a cooling rack. Cut into wedges to serve.

Storage Store in an airtight container or bag for up to 3 days at room temperature.

2½ cups (600 grams) warm water

1 tablespoon (9 grams) active dry yeast

2 tablespoons (28 grams) sugar

3 tablespoons (63 grams) honey

¾ cup (169 grams) vegetable oil

5 cups (650 grams) all-purpose flour

2½ cups (350 grams) einkorn or sorghum flour

1 tablespoon (15 grams) fine sea salt

1½ teaspoons ground cinnamon

1 teaspoon ground green cardamom

½ cup (80 grams) golden raisins

Vegetable oil or cooking spray, for greasing the pan

2 tablespoons milk, for brushing on top

ETHIOPIAN BARBECUE CORN BREAD

Serves 8

Corn is so important to me personally, and to the wider African diaspora in general. The great Southern chef Edna Lewis pioneered the idea of baking corn bread in a hot skillet, and I wanted to pay tribute to her by imbuing her recipe with Ethiopian flavors. Try this savory, spicy corn bread when you need a little something different, especially when you already have Zhoug (page 25) on hand for making the zhoug compound butter.

PREHEAT THE OVEN to 400°F. Place the niter kibbeh in an 8- or 9-inch cast-iron skillet and set in the preheating oven until melted, about 5 minutes.

Swirl the butter around the sides of the pan to coat, then pour the melted niter kibbeh into a large bowl and set aside to cool slightly. Return the skillet to the oven.

Add the buttermilk or milk and egg to the bowl with the butter and whisk lightly to combine.

In a medium bowl, mix the cornmeal, flour, baking powder, baking soda, salt, berbere (if using), and brown sugar. Pour the dry ingredients into the bowl of wet ingredients and fold together until just combined. If the mixture appears dry, add another splash of buttermilk or milk.

Carefully remove the hot cast-iron pan from the oven. Pour the batter into the pan and smooth out the top.

Bake until the corn bread is lightly golden, the top springs back to the touch, and the sides are starting to pull away from the pan, about 30 minutes.

Serve with zhoug butter.

⅓ cup (76 grams) Niter Kibbeh (page 15) or unsalted butter

1 cup (230 grams) buttermilk (for a richer, cakier corn bread) or milk, plus more as needed

1 large egg

1⅓ cups (160 grams) cornmeal

1 cup (130 grams) all-purpose flour

2 teaspoons baking powder

½ teaspoon baking soda

1 teaspoon fine sea salt

½ teaspoon Berbere (page 5; optional, omit for a simpler corn bread)

¼ cup (65 grams) brown sugar (or more for sweeter corn bread)

Spicy Zhoug Butter (page 26), for serving

COLLARD GREENS and CABBAGE BOUREKAS

Makes 12 bourekas (serves about 4)

Israel meets Ethiopia in these bourekas, little flaky pastry pockets filled with cheese, potatoes, or spinach that are very much an Israeli staple. I've filled mine with collard greens and cabbage, spiced as an Ethiopian stew would be, along with sesame, which is grown all over Ethiopia (including in my native Tigray region).

This recipe makes more filling than you'll need for the bourekas: Serve the extra as a stew with your next meal.

The pastry for the bourekas is a "blitz" or "rough puff" dough—it's essentially a standard pie dough that you fold to create laminated, flaky layers of puff pastry. If you would like to skip this step, you can easily use one approximately 8-ounce sheet of frozen puff pastry (I like the Pepperidge Farm brand); see the Note for how to do so. This will result in a thinner pastry crust.

The bourekas can be shaped and frozen, and when you are ready to eat them, just brush them with egg wash and sprinkle them with sesame seeds before popping them straight into a hot oven. If you bake them directly from the freezer, they will take a few minutes longer in the oven.

MAKE THE ROUGH PUFF: In a medium bowl, mix ½ cup plus 1 tablespoon (134 grams) cold water and the lemon juice. Sprinkle the flour and salt over the liquid and place the butter pieces on top. Use a spatula or your hands to gently mix the dough just until it comes together into a shaggy dough, keeping the large butter chunks intact. Press the dough together, wrap it in plastic wrap, and refrigerate for at least 30 minutes or up to 12 hours.

On a floured surface, roll the dough out to an 11 × 9-inch rectangle (roughly the size of a standard sheet of paper). With a long side facing you, fold the right side in toward the center, then the left side over the right side just as you would fold a letter. This is your first fold. With a short side facing you, roll out again to a 11 × 9-inch rectangle and complete a second fold. Wrap tightly in plastic wrap and rest in the fridge for another 30 minutes.

ROUGH PUFF

- 1 teaspoon fresh lemon juice
- 2 cups (280 grams) all-purpose flour, plus more for dusting
- 1 teaspoon fine sea salt
- 15 tablespoons (210 grams) cold unsalted butter, cut into tablespoon-sized chunks

BOUREKA FILLING

- 2 medium potatoes, cut into 1-inch cubes
- 4 tablespoons Niter Kibbeh (page 15), butter, or cooking oil of your choice
- ½ red onion, chopped
- 2 tablespoons minced fresh ginger
- 4 garlic cloves, minced
- 1 jalapeño, seeded and chopped
- 1 large bunch collard greens, stems and midribs removed, leaves chopped
- 2 cups chopped green cabbage
- 1½ tablespoons Berbere (page 5)
- 1 teaspoon cumin seeds
- ¼ teaspoon ground cardamom
- 1 teaspoon fine sea salt, plus more to taste
- Grated zest of 1 lemon

ASSEMBLY

- 1 egg
- 2–3 tablespoons sesame seeds, for topping

Collard Greens and Cabbage Bourekas continues

Repeat the back-to-back folds one more time, wrap tightly in the plastic wrap, and rest for 30 more minutes.

Make the boureka filling: In a medium pot, combine the potatoes with cold water to cover and bring to a boil over medium-high heat. Cook until the potatoes are tender, about 15 minutes. Drain and rinse with cold water.

In a medium skillet, melt the niter kibbeh over medium heat. Add the onion and sauté until it begins to soften and turn translucent, about 2 minutes. Add the ginger, garlic, and jalapeño and sauté until the raw scent is gone, about 3 minutes. Add the collards, cabbage, berbere, cumin seeds, cardamom, salt, and a few tablespoons of water. Reduce the heat to medium-low and cook, stirring periodically, until the collards and cabbage are tender, 15 to 20 minutes.

Add the potatoes and mash with a potato masher until they are creamy. Add the lemon zest. Taste and add salt if necessary. Remove from the heat and cool completely.

To assemble: Place the dough on a lightly floured surface and roll into a 15-inch square. Cut the dough into 12 equal parts, about 5 × 3¾ inches each. Don't worry if the pastry is not perfectly even on the edges, but it should resemble a rough square.

Beat the egg and have a pastry brush nearby. Have your filling nearby and line a sheet pan with parchment paper. Working with one pastry square at a time, brush the bottom half of the pastry lightly with egg wash. Spoon 1 to 2 tablespoons of filling into the center and pull the top half over the bottom, pressing the sides closed with your fingers or a fork. If the filling is seeping through the closure, open the pastry up and remove some filling. Do not overfill the bourekas or they will pop open in the oven. Place the bourekas 2 inches apart on the prepared sheet pan. If it is hot in your kitchen, you can keep the pastry squares cold in the fridge so they are easier to work with.

Once all the bourekas are shaped and on the sheet pan, cover them tightly with plastic and refrigerate them for at least 30 minutes or until you are ready to bake them. This is also the step at which you can freeze the bourekas for future use. If freezing, cover with plastic until frozen and then transfer to a freezer-safe plastic bag or container.

Preheat the oven to 350°F.

Brush the bourekas with the egg wash and generously sprinkle with sesame seeds. Bake until puffed and golden, 35 to 45 minutes.

Serve warm or at room temperature.

Note If using store-bought puff pastry: Thaw in the refrigerator. Place one sheet (225 grams or ½ pound) on a lightly floured surface and roll out slightly until the rectangle is about 12 × 16 inches. Soften the creases where the pastry was folded. Cut the pastry into 12 equal pieces roughly the size of a Post-it note, using the folds to guide your cuts. Then proceed with filling the bourekas.

MA'ARN TZAVA CAKE / *UGAT HA-LAV OO D'VASH*

Honey Cake

Serves 10 to 12

The Torah calls Israel "the land of milk and honey," and that theme ran through many of the stories that I heard growing up. But so many of my relatives have memories of honey from Ethiopia as well: Many of our families had beehives on their properties. The sweet scent of honey wafts through all the memories that my distant cousin, Vered Germay (page 8), has from her childhood in Ethiopia. She remembers her childhood on the family farm, playing with her brown-and-white dog, Koorchit, amid the dozens of beehives on their property. Most of all, she remembers sneaking into her family's storage room, dipping her finger into a pot of honey, and savoring the sweetness. This cake is my tribute to all things honey, all around the world: I love it for breakfast and dessert. I've given it Ethiopian flair with a bit of coffee extract.

Unsalted butter or cooking spray, for the baking pan

STREUSEL

- 1 cup (145 grams) raw almonds
- ⅓ cup (67 grams) sugar
- ¼ cup (85 grams) honey
- ½ teaspoon fine sea salt
- ¾ cup (105 grams) all-purpose flour
- 1 stick (4 ounces/113 grams) unsalted butter, melted and cooled slightly

CAKE

- 1¾ cups (245 grams) all-purpose flour
- 1 teaspoon baking soda
- 1 teaspoon baking powder
- 1 teaspoon fine sea salt
- 1 stick (4 ounces/113 grams) unsalted butter, at room temperature
- ½ cup (100 grams) sugar
- ½ cup (170 grams) honey
- 2 large eggs, at room temperature
- 1 teaspoon vanilla extract
- 1 tablespoon Ethiopian Coffee Extract (page 33)
- 1 cup (245 grams) plain whole-milk yogurt

PREHEAT THE OVEN to 350°F. Grease a 9 × 13-inch baking pan.

Make the streusel: In a food processor, process the almonds into a coarse meal, about 2 minutes. Add the sugar, honey, and salt and pulse for 30 seconds. Add the flour and pulse while streaming the melted butter into the food processor. Set aside.

Make the cake: In a medium bowl, sift together the flour, baking soda, baking powder, and salt.

In a stand mixer fitted with the paddle, cream the butter and sugar on medium speed until light in color and fluffy, about 4 minutes. Scrape down the bowl with a spatula. Add the honey and mix until incorporated. Add the eggs one at a time, scraping down the bowl in between, until they are both incorporated. Add the vanilla and coffee extract. Reduce the mixer speed to the lowest setting and add the flour mixture, then the yogurt, just until mixed.

Spread the batter into the pan and use an offset spatula to flatten the surface. Spread the streusel across the cake batter, breaking up some of the crumbs and keeping others large.

Bake until golden brown, 35 to 40 minutes.

Cool the cake completely in the pan before cutting.

Storage Cover and keep at room temperature for up to 4 days.

SHAHI-SPICED PRALINE BABKA

Serves 8 to 12

Babka, a stunning braided sweet bread, is an Ashkenazi specialty that I've always loved. My contribution here is to add a praline shahi mix (that I also love on its own). Making the babka can be broken up over two days. You can make the praline paste and shahi spice mix several days in advance. Keep the praline paste refrigerated and bring to room temperature before shaping the babka. The brioche dough can be made a day in advance and proofed overnight in the fridge. Additionally, you can fully shape the babkas and refrigerate them overnight—this method will require a longer final proof, closer to 4 hours.

MAKE THE BABKA DOUGH: In a small microwave-safe bowl, warm the milk in the microwave until it is lukewarm. Sprinkle the yeast over the milk and let sit for 5 minutes to activate the yeast.

In a medium bowl, mix the flour, sugar, and salt.

In a stand mixer fitted with the dough hook, combine the eggs and milk/yeast mixture. Mix on low speed until combined, about 1 minute. Add the dry ingredients, increase the speed to medium, and mix until a dough is formed, 6 to 8 minutes. The dough will not pull away from the sides of the bowl at this point. Let the dough rest in the bowl for 10 minutes.

With the mixer on medium speed, add one piece of butter at a time, and beat until all the butter has been incorporated and the dough is shiny and elastic, 10 to 15 minutes. (You can also mix by hand, which will take 15 to 20 minutes.)

Oil a medium bowl. Shape the dough into a ball, place it in the oiled bowl, cover with plastic wrap, and let rise at room temperature until doubled in size, about 1 hour.

Make the praline filling: Preheat the oven to 350°F. Line a large sheet pan with parchment paper.

Spread the hazelnuts on one side of the sheet pan and the walnuts and pistachios on the other side. Bake, stirring halfway through, until toasted, 8 to 10 minutes.

Place the hazelnuts on a clean kitchen towel. Rub them with the towel to remove as much of the skins as possible.

BABKA DOUGH

- ¼ cup (60 grams) whole milk
- 2 teaspoons active dry yeast
- 2 cups (280 grams) bread flour
- 3 tablespoons (38 grams) sugar
- 2 teaspoons fine sea salt
- 3 large eggs, at room temperature
- 1 stick (4 ounces/113 grams) unsalted butter, cut into 8 tablespoon-sized pieces, at room temperature
- Avocado oil or another neutral oil, for greasing the bowl

PRALINE FILLING

- ¾ cup (100 grams) skin-on hazelnuts
- ¾ cup (70 grams) walnuts
- ½ cup (80 grams) pistachios
- 1 cup (200 grams) sugar
- ½ teaspoon fine sea salt
- 1 tablespoon avocado oil or another neutral oil
- 3 tablespoons (42 grams) unsalted butter, at room temperature

SHAHI SPICE MIX

- ½ teaspoon green cardamom seeds, ground
- 1 teaspoon ground cinnamon
- ⅛ teaspoon grated nutmeg
- ½ teaspoon ground cloves
- ¾ teaspoon ground ginger

ASSEMBLY

- Softened butter, for the loaf pan
- 1 egg
- 2 tablespoons honey

Line a small sheet pan with parchment paper and lightly oil the sides of the tray. Place all the nuts on the pan.

In a medium saucepan, combine the sugar and 2 tablespoons water and heat over medium-low heat, swirling the pan so that the sugar melts evenly, until the sugar is fully melted, about 4 minutes. Pour a little more water into a small bowl and have a pastry brush nearby to brush any sugar crystals off the sides of the pan. Increase the heat to medium-high and continue swirling the pan until the caramel has reached a deep amber color and smells toasted, about 2 minutes. Pour the caramel evenly over the mixed nuts (it may not cover all of them) and let cool completely.

Break up the cooled praline and place in a food processor. Add the salt and oil and process until a paste forms, about 4 minutes. Add the butter and process until incorporated, about 1 minute. Transfer to an airtight container and store at room temperature until you are ready to assemble the babka.

Make the shahi spice mix: In a small bowl, mix the spices together. Set aside until you are ready to assemble the babka.

To assemble: Butter an 8- or 9-inch loaf pan and set aside.

On a lightly floured surface, roll the babka dough into a thin 12 × 18-inch rectangle, taking care that it does not stick to the counter. If the dough is shrinking back before the desired size is reached, let it relax for a moment before continuing. With a short side facing you, spread the praline filling all over the dough in a thin, even layer, stopping about 1 inch from the top of the rectangle. (You may have some left over.)

Sprinkle the shahi spice mix over the praline paste.

Working from the short end, roll the dough away from you into a tight jelly roll. Place the roll on a tray and freeze for 20 minutes to firm the dough.

Using a serrated knife, cut the log in half lengthwise, exposing the entire interior of the log. Press the two strips together at one end and then twist them over each other tightly, pressing the ends together when fully braided. Carefully place the babka in the loaf pan, tucking the ends underneath at each end. Cover with a clean towel or plastic wrap and let proof at room

Shahi-Spiced Praline Babka continues

temperature until puffed and risen to the height of the loaf pan, 2 to 4 hours.

Preheat the oven to 350°F.

In a small bowl, beat the egg, then use a pastry brush to brush it over the top of the babka. Place the loaf pan on a sheet pan.

Bake for 30 minutes. Cover with foil and bake until browned and an instant-read thermometer inserted in the middle reads 200°F, 10 to 20 minutes.

In a small pan, whisk the honey and 2 tablespoons water over low heat until a light syrup forms. Brush the syrup over the hot babka, which will help preserve its moisture. Let cool completely before cutting.

Storage Store in an airtight container at room temperature for up to 1 week.

CARROT COCONUT GINGER CELEBRATION CAKE

Serves 8 to 12

Carrot cake is popular in my husband's Caribbean culture, and it resonates with me when it's not too sweet, packed with fresh carrots, and showered with coconut. Two types of ginger, fresh and dried, give it extra character.

PREHEAT THE OVEN TO 350°F.

Spread the coconut in a single layer on a sheet pan. Toast in the oven, stirring occasionally, until lightly golden, 10 to 15 minutes. Set the coconut topping aside to cool completely. Leave the oven on.

Make the cake: Grease two 8- or 9-inch round cake pans.

Pour the avocado oil into a small bowl and set it next to the stove. In a small pan, melt the butter over medium heat. Cook, stirring and scraping the bottom of the pan constantly, until the butter browns. As the butter gets closer to browning, bubbles and foam will appear on the top and it will smell nutty. When it begins to turn a deep golden color, immediately remove it from the heat and stir it into the oil: This will stop the cooking so the butter does not burn. Set aside until cooled slightly but not solidified, about 20 minutes.

In a medium bowl, sift together the flour, sugar, baking soda, cinnamon, nutmeg, ground ginger, and salt.

In a stand mixer fitted with the paddle, beat the eggs until foamy, about 3 minutes. With the mixer running, stream in the brown butter/oil mixture. Follow with the vanilla and beat until combined. Turn the mixer to low speed and gradually add the flour mixture until just combined. Turn off the machine and fold in the carrots and fresh ginger by hand, until just combined.

Divide the batter evenly between the cake pans, smoothing the tops with a spatula.

Bake until each cake springs back to the touch and is pulling away from the sides of the pan, and a tester comes out clean, 30 to 40 minutes.

2 cups (200 grams) unsweetened shredded coconut

CAKE

Unsalted butter or cooking spray, for greasing the pans

¼ cup (60 grams) avocado oil (or any neutral oil of your choice)

12 tablespoons (6 ounces/ 180 grams) unsalted butter, cut into cubes

2 cups (280 grams) all-purpose flour

1½ cups (300 grams) sugar

2 teaspoons baking soda

1 teaspoon ground cinnamon

¼ teaspoon ground nutmeg

¼ teaspoon ground ginger

1 teaspoon fine sea salt

4 large eggs, at room temperature

1 teaspoon vanilla extract

1½ pounds (680 grams) carrots, shredded

1″ piece fresh ginger, peeled and grated

FROSTING

1 pound (450 grams) cream cheese, at room temperature

1 stick (4 ounces/113 grams) unsalted butter, at room temperature

1 cup powdered sugar

1 teaspoon vanilla extract

Carrot Coconut Ginger Celebration Cake continues

Let the cakes cool in the pans for about 20 minutes, then flip them onto a cooling rack to cool completely.

Make the frosting: In a stand mixer fitted with the paddle, mix the cream cheese and butter on medium-low speed until well combined, about 2 minutes. Add the powdered sugar and mix until the frosting looks light and airy, about 3 minutes. Add the vanilla and mix until combined.

Place the first cake layer on a serving plate. Spread about one-third of the frosting onto the top of the cake, reaching all the way to the edges, and use an offset spatula or table knife to smooth it flat. Place the other cake layer onto the frosted layer and add half of the remaining frosting, pushing the excess down to begin covering the sides of the cake. Use the rest of the frosting to completely cover the top and sides of the cake.

Sprinkle the toasted coconut on the top and lightly press as much as possible onto the sides of the cake (you may have some left over).

NEGESTI SABA CHOCOLATE CARDAMOM CAKE

Queen of Sheba Chocolate Cardamom Cake

Serves 8 to 12

Julia Child's Reine de Saba cake, a beautiful mixture of chocolate and almond, is very French, and named for the Queen of Sheba. I wanted to honor the very same queen—who is known as Makeda throughout Ethiopia, and as Negesti Saba in my native Tigray—and I also wanted to pay tribute to the American culinary legend herself, whom I admire for introducing so many Americans to French cuisine. This is my own version of this landmark cake, which includes the quintessentially Ethiopian ingredients of coffee, teff flour, and korarima (Ethiopian cardamom). It's moist and light, and I hope it helps elevate Ethiopian cuisine just as Julia's version did for French food.

MAKE THE CAKE: Preheat the oven to 350°F. Butter an 8- or 9-inch springform pan.

Pour 2 inches of water into a medium pot and place a heatproof metal bowl on top to make a double boiler. Add the chocolate to the bowl and set the pot over medium heat. Stir with a spatula until the chocolate is melted, 3 to 5 minutes. Remove from the heat and remove the bowl from the pot and set it on the counter. Keep the pot of water handy for the cake glaze later.

In a stand mixer fitted with the whisk, mix the egg whites and a pinch of salt on medium-high speed until they are frothy and lose their yellow tinge, 1 to 2 minutes. Add 1½ tablespoons of the sugar and whisk on high until moderate peaks appear, 1 to 2 minutes. You can check the status of the whites by stopping the machine, removing the whisk, and holding it upright. The peak of the whites should be loose enough to *just* fall over. Transfer the meringue to a medium bowl. Wash and dry the stand mixer bowl.

Fit the stand mixer with the paddle. Cream the butter and the remaining 1 cup sugar on medium speed until light and fluffy, scraping the bottom of the bowl as necessary, about 3 minutes.

Add the yolks to the butter and sugar mixture and mix, scraping the bottom of the bowl as needed, until well incorporated. Stream

CAKE

Softened butter, for the pan

6 ounces (171 grams) dark chocolate (around 70% cacao), chopped

5 large eggs, separated into whites and yolks, at room temperature

A pinch plus ½ teaspoon fine sea salt

1½ tablespoons (22 grams) plus 1 cup (200 grams) sugar

12 tablespoons (6 ounces/170 grams) unsalted butter, at room temperature

2 tablespoons Ethiopian Coffee Extract (page 33)

¼ teaspoon almond extract

⅓ cup (45 grams) almond meal

¾ teaspoon Ground Roasted Korarima (page 26) or ground green cardamom

½ teaspoon ground cinnamon

⅓ cup (45 grams) teff flour (see Note)

CHOCOLATE GLAZE AND TOPPING

3 ounces (85 grams) dark chocolate (around 70% cacao)

3 tablespoons (42 grams) unsalted butter

Whipped cream or vanilla ice cream, for serving

½ cup ground pistachios (optional)

Large pinch of sea salt (optional)

Negesti Saba Chocolate Cardamom Cake continues

in the melted chocolate, stirring constantly, then stir in the coffee extract and almond extract. Add the almond meal, korarima, cinnamon, and ½ teaspoon salt, and mix.

Remove the bowl from the mixer. Add one-third of the teff flour, folding it in with a rubber spatula. Then add one-third of the meringue, carefully folding it in completely by sweeping the spatula across the bottom of the bowl and folding the batter toward you, but being careful not to deflate the volume of the meringue. Continue alternating these additions until all the teff and meringue have been folded into the batter and no white is visible. Pour the batter into the prepared springform pan and smooth out the top.

Bake until the cake is pulling away from the sides of the pan but is still fudgy in the middle, 25 to 30 minutes.

Let it cool completely before glazing. The cake will deflate as it cools.

Meanwhile, make the chocolate glaze: Place the chocolate in the same bowl you used to melt the chocolate for the cake. Heat over the pot of water until melted and then remove from the heat.

Add the butter and stir until it has fully melted. Remove the ring of the springform pan and using two spatulas, carefully move the cake onto a serving plate.

Pour one-third of the chocolate glaze over the top of the cake. Use an offset spatula or table knife to smooth it out and down the sides, adding the remaining glaze, until the cake is covered and smoothed out. The chocolate will begin to harden as you are doing this. Serve with whipped cream or vanilla ice cream. If desired, sprinkle generously with ground pistachios and a pinch of sea salt.

Storage Leftovers can be covered and stored at room temperature for 3 days.

Note Substitute cake flour or gluten-free flour of your choice for the teff flour. You can also replace it with more almond meal, if desired.

CHAPTER 8

HOLIDAYS, CELEBRATIONS, RITUALS, AND MENUS

At the heart of Beta Israel culture are the prayers, chants, and foods with which we celebrate the Old Testament, our pasts, and our futures. In this chapter, you'll learn about our most cherished traditions, and our menus for celebrating them.

SHABBAT

SHABBAT

We believe that Shabbat is the queen, and God is the king. When the sun goes down on Friday night, the Shabbat queen enters, and for the next twenty-four hours, until the sun goes down on Saturday evening, business as usual goes out the window. It is a blessed day of joy, relaxation, and enjoyment, when we avoid all daily labor, such as cooking, cleaning, or traveling. Whether it's called K'edaam in Tigrinya, or Senbat in Amharic, we believe that if you observe this sacred day, Shabbat will protect you from anything.

Throughout this book, you will see examples of how important Shabbat is to Beta Israel: how we observe it even in the most perilous of circumstances and at great personal cost.

Shabbat is so important that we even have a book, Teezaza Senbt, devoted to its laws and rituals. And while Beta Israel eat mostly vegetable choices during the week, we mark the Shabbat with our best meat dishes.

The flurry of excitement starts each Thursday, when mothers and daughters in Ethiopian Jewish homes begin to prepare the Shabbat meal: cleaning chicken in lemon and salt, making injera from scratch, putting together batches of honey wine and beer, and baking dabo.

Once we reached Israel—and many people, like me, subsequently scattered across the globe—the particular dishes may have changed, but not the spirit of Shabbat: It's still a protected, cherished time for so many of us.

MENU

FRIDAY NIGHT

SATURDAY BREAKFAST

PORTRAIT

GENET (ILANA) MAMAY
A Harrowing Journey

My aunt Genet Mamay—*Genet* is Tigrinya for "Paradise"—spent her early childhood in the village of Walkeit, a thriving Beta Israel community in southern Ethiopia where each Friday, families banded together to bake different types of dabo in anticipation of resting together on the Shabbat. Her family made their dabo

by placing the dough in a ceramic pot and burying it in hot coals and wood. They roasted their coffee beans over the same fire, the green beans turning dark from the heat.

Her name, "Paradise," reflected not only Genet's own promise but also the hope that she and her family might travel to the promised land of Israel. And travel they did, but neither Genet nor her parents could have prepared for what they would have to give up in the process: Their safety. Their identities. And their hopes that their new country would immediately embrace them as fellow members of the Jewish faith.

Genet had grown up hearing tales of the land of milk and honey from her aunt Yeshu Tesfay. "Israel is truly the place for us," her aunt constantly told her while preparing the family for the journey. When Genet was ten, she and her family and dozens of others in their Beta Israel community left their village, en route to Sudan. It began as a beautiful, joyful walk, along rivers that provided water and a place for the children to splash around. Fruit trees provided abundant nourishment, and along the way, the adults were able to make bread and coffee over fires.

Unfortunately, things took a tragic turn on the third day of their journey. A new mother, carrying her baby on her back, collapsed and died. The rest of the group had no choice but to bury her where they were and keep going.

Still reeling from the tragedy, the group was heartened to encounter some friendly villagers herding cows and goats, who chatted with the travelers and even offered them milk. Little did the travelers know that those villagers hid a sinister motive: They intended to turn them in to the Derg, the Ethiopian military junta that prohibited families from leaving the country.

Genet's group was blindsided by the sound of gunshots. "Do not run," the officers shouted, "or we're going to kill you." Genet and her family panicked as they watched some of their fellow travelers fall to the ground, injured. Others managed to outrun the officers, disappearing from the chaos. But most of the group, including Genet's family, had no choice but to raise their hands and surrender.

In the following nightmarish days, the family had to hand over all the jewelry that had been passed down for generations and safely packed for the long journey—now never to be seen again. They were forced to relinquish all the money they had saved for the trip. And they were locked into an old compound, interrogated and slapped around for hours, and given flour as their only sustenance.

Thankfully, the Derg then abandoned them, and one of the travelers managed to escape from the compound and locate her husband on the outside. With his help, the remaining travelers eventually escaped, and were able to make their way to a Sudanese refugee camp.

After three months in the camp—during which they left only to buy water—Genet's uncle managed to get word of their escape to Ferede Aklum (page xxxi). Aklum quickly snapped into action, collaborating with the Mossad to get the group passports to leave the country. And one day, a pile of passports arrived, allowing the group to travel through Greece to Israel. There was one for each traveler: Genet, her parents, her siblings, her uncle, her cousins— her. Yeshu waited in Sudan for her passport. But before it arrived, she fell ill and died there, never having seen the land of milk and honey that she had so passionately promised Genet.

Arriving at the Israeli airport was the first time that Genet had ever seen people who were not Black. After airport officials saw that the group was Black, they assumed they needed to convert to Judaism, and they were ordered to bathe in a mikvah, a ritual that greatly insulted the devout Beta Israel family. Finally, they were given new Israeli names at random. Genet became Ilana.

"All of my dreams kind of disappeared," Genet remembers. While at the time, she embraced being called Ilana, she now wishes that she had been able to keep her meaningful birth name.

When Genet was in seventh grade, she went away for boarding school. Many Ethiopian Jewish teenagers did so, to learn the language and integrate into Israeli society, and to create some distance between them and their families. Many of our Israeli teachers encouraged this as a way to make us independent.

In reality, this practice created more than just physical distance. It also created a distance between generations, and a sense of embarrassment and shame in the families whose parents did not understand the local language or customs, and watched as their children drifted further from their Ethiopian roots.

Once Genet went to boarding school, she also experienced a common form of discrimination toward the Beta Israel community: Our Israeli instructors recommended that we veer toward vocational classes, not academic ones. They often told us that the best thing for us was to learn a vocation, get a job, and integrate into Israeli society. It didn't seem to occur to them that we could achieve anything academically.

I admire Genet because she pushed against this discrimination and became very academically driven. She attended a religious

GENET'S DISHES

school for girls, and got an excellent education from many teachers, including one who had survived the Holocaust. By understanding her worth, pushing against expectations, *and* remaining close to her family, Genet made the most of her time at boarding schools.

Genet eventually settled in Bet Shemesh, Israel. She became a dental hygienist, married my mother's youngest brother, Avraham, and bore five children. She fused much of her traditional Ethiopian cooking with Israeli influences: For instance, her Dubba Wot (page 113) contains silan, a date honey that is popular in Israel.

Throughout her life, Genet has always observed Shabbat as a protected, cherished time during which no work is done. "Even though my kids are out of the house, I always make sure they all come for a meal on a Saturday. That makes me so happy." Each Friday, in anticipation of Shabbat, Genet bakes a fragrant, spice-infused shabbat dabo (see Nay Kedam Dabo, page 51) similarly to how she remembers doing as a child in Walkeit—in a pot on the stove. This method creates a gorgeous, bronzed bread with a hint of smoke and heady undertones of fenugreek, coriander, and cardamom. She turns the bread into Dabo Fit-Fit / Crumbled Dabo with Spices (page 74) each Saturday morning, when her son and daughter-in-law come over for breakfast. The family likes to gather in the garden, snacking on sunflower seeds and nuts, enjoying each other's company, telling stories, and reflecting on the rest of the week. They do not use the TV, phones, or any other electronics.

And they mark the end of the Shabbat by roasting coffee, enjoying the same smells and flavors of Genet's long-ago childhood, memories and rituals that no uniformed officer could take from her.

THE HABESHA COFFEE CEREMONY

As in many Ethiopian homes, when visitors came by, my parents welcomed them with this unique ceremony, which celebrates our birthplace's long-standing coffee culture.

The ceremony's performer—traditionally a woman, but done by men in modern times—begins by burning incense to ward off evil spirits. Then, she roasts the coffee beans. As they begin to burn, she walks around the room, filling it with the smoke. She stops in front of guests and family members alike who have asked for blessings, fanning smoke onto them, as this is considered a blessing of its own.

The boiled coffee is served in a jebena (a ceramic kettle) and poured into ceramic cups beautifully painted with distinctly Ethiopian images and figures. Sometimes, we would even lay freshly cut grass on the floor near where the coffee ceremony was to be performed. This is meant to signify a sacred space, connecting the participants to nature, and emphasizing the earthly origins of coffee.

The coffee is then served in three rounds. The first is called abol. This tends to be the strongest coffee and it is said that it "is served for pleasure." The second is called tona and is slightly weaker than the first, said to "provoke contemplation." The third and final round is called baraka, and is thought to "bestow the blessing."

Each cup of coffee is said to transform the spirit, but the third serving is considered a blessing to those who drink it. Incidentally, because of its diluted nature, this is the same serving in which children can partake.

Snacks of roasted barley, peanuts, popcorn, or bread may accompany the coffee, and guests heap abundant praise on the performer and her brews, while also discussing politics and community gossip.

This unique cultural custom is practiced throughout the Horn of Africa, predominantly in Ethiopia and Eritrea, where it is a sign of respect and friendship to be invited to a coffee ceremony.

The Ethiopian Coffee Legend

As we say to children to begin a tale, Teret Teret Yelam Beret:
Kaldi, an Abyssinian goatherd from Kaffa, was herding his

goats through a highland area near a monastery. He noticed that they were behaving very strangely that day, jumping around in an excited manner, bleating loudly, and practically dancing on their hind legs. The source of the excitement was a small shrub with bright red berries. Curiosity took hold, and Kaldi tried the berries for himself.

Like his goats, he soon felt the energizing effects of the coffee cherries. After filling his pockets with the red berries, he rushed home to his wife, and she advised him to go to the nearby monastery in order to share these "heaven-sent" berries with the monks there.

At the monastery, Kaldi's coffee beans were greeted not with enthusiasm but with disdain. One monk called Kaldi's bounty "the Devil's work" and tossed it into a fire. However, according to legend, the aroma of the roasting beans was enough to make the monks think twice. They removed the coffee beans from the fire, crushed them to put out the glowing embers, and covered them with hot water in order to preserve them: creating the world's first cup of coffee.

To have your own coffee ceremony, see Buna (page 171).

BIRTH

The weeks after an Ethiopian Jewish woman gives birth are considered sacred. We believe that a mother should be given a peaceful sanctuary to heal from childbirth, connect with her child, and rejuvenate herself. This sanctuary is known as the Harrase Gojo ("The House of the New Mother"), where women stay for forty days after the birth of a boy, eighty after the birth of a girl. There the mother is supported by other women who do all her chores, including cooking and laundry. They care for her mental health by talking to her and looking out for any signs of depression, and they guide her on breastfeeding her child.

Meanwhile, the woman's husband and older children are also cared for by members of the community, who take turns bringing them food. When the forty or eighty days are up, the community throws a big feast, welcoming the mother and the newborn home.

I wish I had had that kind of network when I had my children in New York. I was lucky to have had my mother come from Israel to take care of me and make me food. But I know many people who gave birth with few people to support and guide them. This display of community would have improved their lives immeasurably.

DISHES FOR BIRTH

80 Genfo
81 Atmit
177 Telva
64 Hanza

DEATH

My grandmother Bezabish Worku, affectionately known as Babish, was the center of our family. In addition to raising my mother and her siblings, she raised her nieces and nephews after the death of her brother, and she played a large part in raising me as well. Once we immigrated to Israel, her house became the place where everyone gathered, ate, and celebrated.

When Babish became sick, my aunt took her to her house, where she made Hanza (page 64) and porridge for her. In her last days, my grandmother asked for black-eyed peas and barley stew (see page 125) and lovingly said goodbye to our family. She was very spiritual, and didn't suffer or agonize over her impending death. She just knew it was her time to leave. We called her a Tsadikh in Hebrew: a righteous person, who does not suffer and has an easy transition to death.

We Beta Israel believe that when a person dies, they must be wrapped in white cloth by only a few people, and must be buried immediately—or at least as soon as possible. Their body is considered unclean, and anyone who touches it must cleanse.

Their family will mourn during shiva for about seven days, which often consists of sitting on the floor, crying, and remembering the person. Often, the family constructs a tent outside the house—we call it *hazen beit*—where people come with food and drinks—injera, fruit, drinks—to be blessed. After the seventh day, the family leaves the tent and purifies themselves in the river or the mikvah. Some slaughter a sheep to honor the dead.

Traditionally, we commemorate the dead each year with a blessing over dabo.

Ethiopian tradition calls for the mourning to be done at the house or at a synagogue: strict Beta Israel believe cemeteries are unclean, and that visitors to burial grounds should cleanse and purify themselves before returning to their households. However, after we began living in Israel, we did mourn more at cemeteries, following local customs of bringing flowers and washing the graves.

My family commemorates my grandma and my mom every year. I try to tell my kids how important it is to remember your parents and do whatever you can to continue their memory.

DISHES TO COMMEMORATE THE DEAD

WEDDINGS

Weddings are a time of ancient ritual and great celebration. When my family lived in Ethiopia, the first step in a marriage was usually taken by the prospective groom's family. Upon deeming his son an adult who was ready to be married, the groom's father would begin asking around about suitable brides, often surveying women in neighboring villages.

Then the groom's father and other family elders (often a religious leader) would visit the prospective bride's family, who would serve a nice meal and coffee. After the meal, the groom's father would say, "I am here to ask for the hand of your daughter."

The bride's family would in turn reply that they would do their diligence and get back to them. Part of this next stage of vetting involved research into the other family's finances, morals, and adherence to the Torah. It also involved Seven Generation, which traces family lineage back seven generations to ensure that the bride and groom are not blood-related. (If the request ended in a rejection for whatever reason, the groom's family would move on to another family.)

Once the bride's side decided that the groom was a good fit, they would send back a message accepting the proposal and saying that they wanted to further the relationship with the other family. They would set a date for an engagement party at their house, where the groom's family would bring a dowry, and the bride's family would serve a festive meal. At this point, the bride and groom would meet in person, and a wedding date was set: often based around the ending of an important harvest, which would ensure a bounty of food for the wedding celebration.

One of the most beautiful prewedding rituals was that of henna. The ceremony was usually held a few days before the wedding and attended by the bride's female relatives and friends. My cousin Vered Germay (page 8) remembers this celebration as full of dance and music. The ladies were massaged with oils and perfumes, and artists came in to paint intricate designs in henna all over their hands, fingers, legs, and toes.

The culmination of all of this was a festive celebration that lasted for at least seven days. The most important day, the wedding itself, might have included a thousand or more people in a specially built tent called an Adarash (a hall). In many families, the bride and groom would dress in beautiful gowns and ride into the ceremony on horses, while drummers and other live musicians

A MENU FOR A WEDDING

walked with them to the chuppah for the exchange of vows and the blessing. A huge celebration would follow, where the families offered their best dishes, with an emphasis on meat. And the couple's closest friends fed them Gursha with their own hands, symbolizing their love, friendship, respect.

The rest of the week featured smaller parties: often the married couple's first Shabbat, a party for the individual families. Then the couple could begin their life together.

While many of these traditions have faded away—for instance, modern marriages tend to not be arranged—my family's weddings still feature an impressive menu.

ASHENDA / CELEBRATION OF FEMALES

Ashenda, the festival celebrating the creativity, beauty, and empowerment of women and girls, is so dear to my family, not only because of its unique joyfulness and roots in ancient Jewish traditions but also because it is unique to my native Tigray region and still celebrated by Tigray people around the world. (The word *ashenda* is Tigrinya for "tall green grass.")

Ashenda, which often falls around August, is an ancient Jewish/Hebraic custom that goes back to the time of the Second Temple. It was celebrated in the old ways, so its roots are very much ancient Hebraic tradition. Over time, it became popular with Ethiopian Christians (who often made it about the Virgin Mary), but the Beta Israel community strongly believes that given its roots in ancient Jewish tradition, it should be preserved. Once most of the Beta Israel community moved to Israel, they started celebrating it there as well. They hold it in a special hall where all women come dressed beautifully and celebrate, dance, and, of course, eat.

AN ASHENDA MENU

198 Himbasha
71 Kolo
132 Kik Alicha
107 Gomen

PORTRAIT

TERFINISH FEREDE
Above and Beyond

My aunt Terfinish Ferede was born right after her father died, which is how she got her name, which means "you are what remains of him." But my own special name for her reflects the beautiful Ethiopian tradition of giving unique names to your elders. I call her Tamaty, which means a caretaker who goes above and beyond.

Terfinish truly went above and beyond. As we fled Ethiopia en

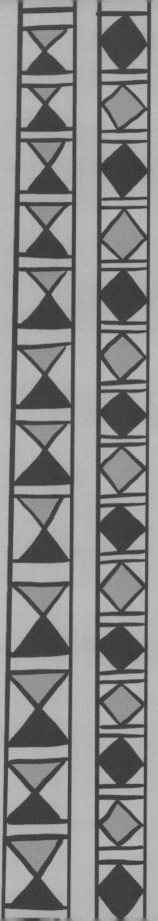

route to Israel, she hoisted four-year-old me on her back and I remained there, my arms slung around her shoulders, for much of the voyage through the Ethiopian desert to Sudan. In Sudan, she helped care for me for the few years we spent in a safe house. She remains one of my most cherished relatives and most meaningful ties to our life in Ethiopia. I find it deeply meaningful to listen to her talk about her fondest memories of our farm in Tigray, as well as her recollections of Ashenda (Celebration of Females), the annual festival that celebrates the female beauty and spirit.

As a young girl, Terfinish recalls running through the family fields of pumpkins and tomatoes, sometimes helping to pick them up and bring them back to the house. She loved to pick fruit off the trees and eat it with water mixed with a little honey. She remembers that all the food they needed was right there: chickens and eggs, and cows that produced milk for butter. Her mother (my grandmother), Bezabish Worku, spotted her talent for accounting and saving money at a young age, and so the family put Terfinish in charge of shopping for any ingredients they did not grow, such as salt and sugar. Terfinish recalls that her mother's talent for making pottery often netted the family unique fruits and vegetables at the market, which they would barter for her bowls and cups.

Terfinish's most moving memories revolve around Ashenda, for which, she says, the preparations started months in advance. Terfinish remembers that some years, she and her friends went to get matching dresses made by a tailor; other years they wore the best dresses they already owned. Terfinish remembers fondly that one year, her godmother bought her beautiful bracelets and earrings to match her dress.

On the morning of Ashenda, Terfinish and her friends dashed down to the river to wash themselves, then put on their dresses. They braided their hair in the special Tigrayan style of five cornrow braids, and all used the same eye makeup, known as kohl koohli.

Together, the girls traveled throughout the village, singing and dancing. Their neighbors welcomed them by spreading green grass to symbolize renewal and blessings, and sometimes the girls would make the grass into a belt or skirt. As the girls danced from household to household, people gave them money, food, clothing. In some cases, more well-to-do neighbors even gave them bigger items, such as a small cow or goat, that they could use for farming or growing their own small business. Often, their brothers accompanied them as a kind of security.

TERFINISH'S DISH

198 Himbasha

Terfinish remembers Ashenda as a time of unification when her family celebrated with neighbors and friends who were Christian and Muslim. It was simply a universal, joyous holiday focused on empowering women and girls to be themselves, be creative, and celebrate their beauty. Even girls who rarely leave the house are given a chance to shine during Ashenda.

Many of my memories of Terfinish revolve around her protecting me throughout my childhood. But when I spoke with her about our shared journey from Ethiopia, the one image that stood out in her head was that of someone she could not protect: our family cow, Sandal.

Sandal was a new mother with two calves, and our family desperately wanted to bring them on our journey, despite the fact that we knew we would be walking through treacherous territory and might not have the resources to care for them. Sandal and her calves walked a good half of the way to Sudan with us until it became clear that we had to just give them away to local villagers. It broke my aunt's heart to see the young calves stumbling along the road, their hooves bleeding from the journey. Though we eventually made it safely, my aunt remains haunted by the thought of the cows we left behind.

BERHAN SERKAN / ROSH HASHANAH

Bowls of ruby-red pomegranate seeds, scallions, apple slices, and honey add splashes of color to Dr. Ephraim Isaac's family table. It's Rosh Hashanah, and Dr. Isaac's family—including three children and four grandchildren—has gathered to mark the occasion together. They bless the Malawach (page 194)—in honor of his ancestral Yemeni roots—and dig into bountiful bowls of Yemenite Chicken Soup (page 159), each with its own whole onion.

Each time he celebrates the Jewish New Year, Dr. Isaac recalls how beautiful his native Ethiopia is during this time of year. "The clouds are moving away. The rain is going, the sunlight is coming up," says Dr. Isaac, who remembers yellow daisies sprouting and filling up the hills near his birthplace.

"It's really a complete change of season. And that change of season is very important in the sense that the New Year then becomes the opening, the beginning of the creation. For everyone. Children go around greeting people, greeting families, maybe bringing flowers or singing some songs. It's a beautiful, beautiful holiday."

Rosh Hashanah—known to Beta Israel as Brenha Serkan or "the emerging of the light"—marks the day the world was created. Depending on the lunar calendar, it typically occurs in September, starting one night at sundown and ending at the next day's sundown—and is a time of hopeful renewal for Jews, who wash away their past sins and dress in white clothes for prayer, family time, and food. Rosh Hashanah is only celebrated for one day by the Beta Israel community—unlike in the West, where it is celebrated for two.

"Rosh Hashanah is really a beautiful holiday," Dr. Isaac said. "The new year has had the particular distinction of being associated with completely new creation. And so you re-create yourself or you renew your sense of humanity. This is a time when there are new seeds being planted. The general feeling of renewal and personal renewal and community family renewal is very important, very significant.

"People come much closer together on that day and families visit with each other and pray for good times to come. A new period of happiness, joy, peace, to come to the world."

A MENU TO CELEBRATE THE NEW YEAR

Rosh Hashanah also marks the beginning of a number of fall holidays celebrated by the Beta Israel:

ENKUTATASH / ETHIOPIAN NEW YEAR

My aunt Shiwaynish Tzgai (page 121) remembers how festive and joyful it was to celebrate the Ethiopian New Year by giving out daisies, exchanging gifts, dancing outside with the neighbors, and eating delicious food. This often falls right around Rosh Hashanah.

ASTERY / YOM KIPPUR

Most other Jews regard Yom Kippur as a quiet, grave day about atonement. And indeed, the Ethiopian Jewish community marks it with a day of fasting. However, our Yom Kippur is fundamentally a happy day—a day filled with rejoicing, chanting, and dancing, a day of redemption and connection when your sins are let go.

It begins with a cleansing of the self: We immerse and wash our clothes in the river, purifying them for the holy day.

My family's Yom Kippur is spiritual and meaningful to everyone, and has evolved throughout the years. Now that they are older, my children fast voluntarily. We have a tradition of placing cloves in a lemon or apple, which is a soothing smell while you fast. Once sundown comes, I often break my fast gently, with mint tea and lentil soup, while my children dive right into a filling meal of fried chicken and red velvet waffles. And we wish each other "Gmar Chatima Tovah"—"May you be sealed in the book of life."

BAA'L MASALAT / SUKKOT / FESTIVAL OF BOOTHS

A celebration to commemorate the booths that the Israelites built when they came out of Egypt. During the seven days of the festival, the Beta Israel community builds a communal dass (shelter, or sukkah in Hebrew). We eat dabo, as well as bounty from the earth, such as cabbage, collard greens, and pomegranates.

BERHAN SERKAN /
ROSH HASHANAH

POR TR AIT

DR. EPHRAIM ISAAC

"Are there really Jews who are Africans? Black Jews?" Dr. Ephraim Isaac was lecturing in a synagogue when he got this question. He certainly had the authority to answer. He is the director of the Institute of Semitic Studies at Princeton University and the chair of the board of the Ethiopian Peace and Development Center. He was raised in Ethiopia by a Yemenite father and an Ethiopian mother, before moving to the United States and marrying an American-born woman from an Ashkenazi family. He is used to this line of questioning while living in a country where Jewish culture and Ashkenazi culture are often treated as one and the same.

He recalls going to a synagogue after moving to the United States. And people said, "Are you Jewish?"

"Yes, I am."

And they said, "But you don't look Jewish."

This treatment particularly stung, he said, because it often came from secular Jewish people who didn't speak Hebrew, knew much less about the religion, and in some cases, rarely went to synagogue.

As Beta Israel, Dr. Isaac and I have faced similar stereotypes and assumptions. I have also found that many assume we Ethiopians were converted to Judaism, perhaps by some kind of white savior.

But Dr. Isaac points out that Hebraic traditions were an integral

DR. ISAAC'S DISHES

part of Ethiopia even before Christianity—and the connection between ancient Israel and Ethiopia goes back to the very early history of the Jewish people. (See Beta Israel History, page xxviii for more.)

Dr. Isaac believes that there is a growing awareness of racial diversity within Judaism. "People have become more educated," he says. The bottom line: "Nobody is more Jewish than anybody else. We have to respect each other. We have to accept each other. That is my philosophy."

SIGD FESTIVAL / MEHELELA

SIGD FESTIVAL / MEHELELA

Melkam Sigd! An ancient holiday that is held seven weeks after Yom Kippur, Sigd memorializes the desire to return to Jerusalem. The first to celebrate it were the prophets Ezra and Nehemiah when they were exiled in Babylon, and the Beta Israel celebrated it, too, when they were yearning for the return to Zion/Jerusalem. Sigd, which often falls around November, commemorates the Covenant that was made when the Torah was given to Moses on Mount Sinai.

It's a unique day that has a little bit of everything. In the morning, Beta Israel fast and many of them carry rocks up the highest mountain in the village, meant to symbolize Mount Sinai. They chant, pray for forgiveness and redemption, and read from the books of Exodus and Psalms. At the top of the mountain, they let go of the rocks, which symbolizes letting go of their sins. In Ethiopia, this was often a time of reunion with people from other regions.

Around midday, people descend the mountain, return to the synagogue, and rejoice with song and delicious food, honoring their holy commitments and giving thanks. Doro wot, dabo, and tej are all on the menu.

Once we moved to Israel, the morning celebrations often involved bussing into Jerusalem for the morning ceremony, then moving home for the celebration.

Some ask: "If it's a holiday for returning, why are we still celebrating it? We made it to Jerusalem." The reason is because we are still praying and waiting to rebuild the Third Temple. Until that happens, we believe that Jews throughout the diaspora and the world should adopt this holiday. It's become a national holiday in Israel and is a wonderful way to celebrate Jewish diversity and unity.

A MENU FOR SIGD

51 Nay Kedam Dabo
153 Kai Wot
143 Doro Wot
45 Doro Wot Alicha
107 Gomen
114 Diniche Alicha
113 Dubba Wot
96 My Mother's Cabbage
64 Hanza
180 Tej
171 Buna

HANUKKAH

The Festival of Lights is such a hopeful, inspirational story, and though Beta Israel do not consider Hanukkah to be a major holiday, I love celebrating it with my children because it is such a showcase of Jewish resilience. I love the symbolism of a small jug of oil lasting eight days.

After my family settled in Israel, I always enjoyed eating the sufganiyot (doughnuts) while lighting the menorah to welcome the gloomy days of winter: Hanukkah often falls around December.

I take great pride in the fact that it was Ethiopians who preserved the First and Second Books of the Maccabees, which tell the story of Hanukkah—how a small group of Jews resisted against the massive, mighty army of Romans and their attempts to convert them. This is an important story to tell in these times.

A HANUKKAH MENU

HANUKKAH

FASSIKAH / PESACH /
WURENAH / PASSOVER

FASSIKAH / PESACH / WURENAH / PASSOVER

The story of Passover deeply resonates with me and my family because it is the story of an exodus. The Israelites escaped slavery in Egypt and walked to freedom. My journey may have had different circumstances, but it was one of similar sacrifice and struggle.

This was a time of great joy and anticipation within the Beta Israel community. Our most unique tradition was breaking the old ceramic dishes from last year—which have absorbed whatever food was cooked or served in them—and welcoming new ones. My grandmother, an expert maker of pottery, would start making new dishes several weeks ahead of Passover: She would make a new large red clay pot, perhaps a long container for honey wine, and often even a new mogogo, the vessel used to make injera.

Then when it came time to cook the Passover meal, our family would hold a ceremony and spiritual blessing. My grandmother would break the old pots, and rejoice in bringing something new to the world. We often butchered a goat, and of course we avoided all leavened bread in favor of a special matzah.

A PASSOVER MENU

ACKNOWLEDGMENTS

Thank you to Tom Pold and the entire Knopf family for believing in this project and patiently providing support

Elisa Ung for helping reach this unbelievable goal

Sally Ekus and her team at the Ekus Group and Jean V. Naggar Literary Agency

Photographer Clay Williams, food stylist Roscoe Betsill, Brittany Conerly, and Uchenna Oobi

Illustrator Eden Yilma

All those who provided encouragement, advice, and support: Julia Turshen, Jake Cohen, Leah Koenig, Julia Bainbridge, Adeena Sussman, Einat Admony, Andy Tepper, Amanda Dell, and The Jewish Food Society

Our recipe testers: David Joachim, Elisheva Charm, Megan Litt, Danielle Brodsky, and Chet Siegel

All those who gave their time to be interviewed and those who helped the process: Dr. Ephraim Isaac and his family, Mali Aklum, Vered Germay, Rishan Mesele, Aster Solomon, Alemash Tessma, Avejo Aklum, Shiwaynish Tzgai, Asefash Mesele, Mehrata Avraham, Terfinish Ferede, and Genet (Ilana) Mamay

My family and friends, for their time, effort, and research, to bring this book to fruition: Padmore John, Alem John, Prestah Berhan Ori John, Nurit Tezazu, Hava Tizazu, Areghey Ferede, Eden Ferede, Zegaye Yossef Tezazu, Berhane Mengesha, Ayodeji Otuyelu, Belynish Teshalle, Yerusalem Work, Ellie Rudee, Joel Mentor, the Tsion Café Team, the Ras Hagos Foods Team, the Tsion Productions Team, the Sheba Tej Team, Jael Sanchez, Anwar Young, Almaz Amine, Elizabeth Dembrowsky, Helen Alefe, and Muliye Gurmu

INDEX

(Page references in *italics* refer to illustrations.)

A NOTE ON THE TYPE

This book was set in Adobe Garamond. Designed for
the Adobe Corporation by Robert Slimbach, the fonts
are based on types first cut by Claude Garamond
(ca. 1480–1561). Garamond was a pupil of Geoffroy Tory
and is believed to have followed the Venetian models,
although he introduced a number of important differences,
and it is to him that we owe the letter we now know as
"old style." He gave to his letters a certain elegance and
feeling of movement that won their creator an immediate
reputation and the patronage of Francis I of France.

Composed by North Market Street Graphics
Lancaster, Pennsylvania

Printed and bound by RRD China
Guangdong, China

Designed by Anna B. Knighton

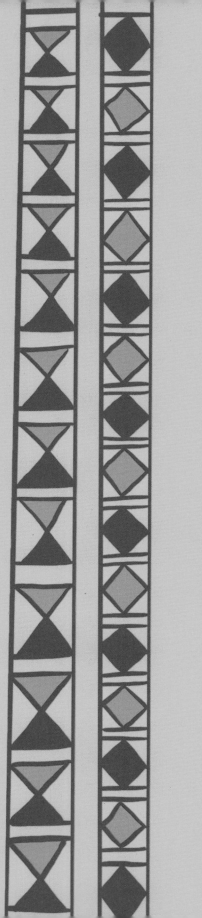